1001 Ways to Save Money... and Still Have a Dazzling Wedding

SHARON NAYLOR

CB
CONTEMPORARY BOOKS

Library of Congress Cataloging-in-Publication Data

Naylor, Sharon.
    1001 ways to save money — and still have a dazzling
wedding / Sharon Naylor.
      p.   cm.
    ISBN 0-8092-3657-5
    1. Weddings.   I. Title.   II. Title: Thousand and one ways
to save money — and still have a dazzling wedding.
BJ2051.N39   1994
395'.22—dc20   94-20718
                                          CIP

For Ron

Cover illustration by Steve Gillig

Published by Contemporary Books
A division of NTC/Contemporary Publishing Group, Inc.
4255 West Touhy Avenue, Lincolnwood (Chicago), Illinois 60712-1975 U.S.A.
Copyright © 1994 by Sharon Naylor
Printed in the United States of America
International Standard Book Number: 0-8092-3657-5
00 01 02 03 04 05 QP 26 25 24 23 22 21 20 19 18 17 16 15 14 13 12 11 10

Contents

Acknowledgments

I have to thank my indispensable panel of brides for their survey responses and their suggestions. Among these outstanding women and wonderful friends are three very special inspirations: Jill Althouse-Wood, Pamela Bishop, and Karen Beyke.

Of course, much gratitude goes to my agent, Elizabeth Frost Knappman, for her dedication and support.

And it goes without saying that Andy and Joanne Blahitka are master wedding planners and phenomenal parents.

Preface

Ever since you were a young girl, you have undoubtedly imagined your wedding. You saw yourself in a beautiful white princess gown dancing with your handsome, tuxedoed husband in a grand ballroom filled with crystal chandeliers, flowers, and ice sculptures. A string quartet is playing classical selections to your five hundred guests, who sip happily at their Dom Pérignon and enjoy an eight-course meal, and then you and your husband are whisked off in a shiny, white stretch limousine for a month-long Hawaiian honeymoon.

Every daydream produced a new addition to your

lifelong dream of the perfect wedding you'd surely have. Princess Diana's big day inspired you to add a long train to your fantasy gown and—why not?—a ride in a horse-drawn carriage to the ceremony. Your Cousin Emily's wedding, while not quite as lofty as Di's, made you want the same kind of seven-tier chocolate ganache cake and an international coffee bar for your own reception.

And now here you are, planning your own wedding at last. You've lined up every detail of the wedding you have in mind, and when you're done with the grave task of pricing everything, you find that you could purchase an airline (or at least pay off your college loans) for what it would cost to put together your Big Day at today's prices. Reality hits, and it'll take the wind out of any bride and groom. As it seems, you'll have to either drain your life savings, cash in your savings bonds and insurance policies, sell your cars, or wear protective headgear when you ask your parents for that ungodly amount of money OR you can start looking for ways to save money on your wedding. It seems that you've already decided on the latter. Good choice.

Money, unfortunately, is a very large part of the planning of a wedding. The entire matrimonial industry revolves around it, in-laws squabble with the bride and groom about it, and practically every choice you'll make depends on it. But you don't have to have every aspect of your wedding controlled by a dollar sign.

Instead, you can take control of the dollar sign by following the money-saving suggestions in this book. Then your ten-thousand-dollar wedding (or your five-thousand-dollar wedding or your fifty-thousand-dollar wedding) can be had for half that amount—if not less—and if you do it right, no one will be able to tell you saved any money at all.

With the help of this book, you'll learn how to have a less expensive wedding without having a cheap-looking wedding. You'll learn exactly where you should and shouldn't cut corners, how to help your family and bridal party save money, where to seek out free assistance, and how to keep from feeling as if you're short-changing yourself and your wishes just to save a few (thousand) bucks. With the money you've saved, you can start your new life together in a better position financially. (And you get to keep your car!)

Introduction:
General Cost-Cutting Rules

A panel of brides married between 1991 and the present have compiled this list of general rules regarding saving money during the planning of a wedding. Keep these points in mind as you go through the rest of the book—many will apply to more than one area of your planning process:

• "Don't let the money make you crazy. There will always be a cheaper choice than the one you've made, and the bills will pile up. It's a fact of life avoidable only through elopement. This is supposed to be an enjoyable time for you, so don't let figures and totals take away from the total wedding experience."

• "Don't let money be the main topic of conversation when you're talking to your fiancé and family about the planning. Instead of harping on and on about how the bouquets cost this much, focus instead on how beautiful the ceremony is going to be."

• "Don't be cheap. You must indulge in some things for yourself because you are the bride and you do deserve special treatment on your wedding day. So instead of knocking out all luxuries, allow a few for yourself . . . and don't feel guilty about it."

• "Ask your friends how they saved money on their weddings. They may be able to refer you to cost-saving resources you wouldn't otherwise have found."

• "When kind relatives and friends ask to contribute their services, accept their offers. It makes them feel like a special part of your day, and it certainly helps your budget."

• "Speak up about group discounts and be daring enough to try to talk down the price. Your bravery just may earn 10 percent or so off your bill."

• "Speak up if you're not happy with an item or service. If you've ordered something and it arrives in bad condition, stand up for yourself and demand its replacement or a refund. That's a basic of good money management, not just a wedding particular."

• "Try to save money not just for yourself, but for your family, the groom's family, the bridal party, and guests who will be coming to town for your wedding. Your choices do affect each of them financially, and your efforts to cut down the amounts they will have to spend will surely result in less tension and more gratitude."

• "Don't let professionals pressure you into immediate spending. Keep in mind that they may be motivated more by their 25 percent commission than by your happiness. Make the professionals wait for you to decide, so you'll have a chance to find greater savings instead of giving in to impulsive spending."

• "Don't consider the barter system beneath you. If you make a deal with your best friend that her wedding gift to you will be her performance of a song at the ceremony or doing the calligraphy for your wedding programs, she's honored to be a part of your wedding celebration and you've combined a special and memorable gesture with a coincidentally cost-effective plan. There's nothing shameful about that."

• "Why pay for overpriced service when you can do it yourself?"

• "The best parts of any wedding celebration are the personal touches added by the bride and groom: saying your own vows, singing to one another at the ceremony, decorating your reception with pictures and items special to the two of you. All meaning, no price."

1

Your Engagement Announcements

The Newspaper Announcement

Submit your announcement and picture to newspapers that do not charge for publication in their announcement column.

If your town newspaper charges by the word, practice writing your announcement in the fewest words possible. One bride saved fifteen dollars just by revising and condensing.

If your town newspaper charges a flat fee for the announcement itself, get your money's worth by writing a long entry filled with details as an even better memento.

If you'd like to put your announcement in several newspapers and all charge printing fees, choose only the most important ones. These may be papers in your hometown, the groom's hometown, and those of both sets of parents.

If you'd like to put your announcements in several papers and none of them charge printing fees, send your article and picture to newspapers in each of the following towns: yours, the groom's, your parents', his parents', your grandparents', your old hometowns, and your college alumni newspaper.

Keep in mind, though, that even though it may be free to have the article printed in the paper, you'll still have to deal with the expense of picture copies and postage. These can add up.

Edit your engagement announcement well. You don't want to allow typographical errors on your part to be printed in the paper, insulting your future in-laws whose names you've misspelled and causing you to have to pay for an edited version of your announcement in the paper the following week.

Always be sure to put your name and telephone number on the back of the picture you're submitting with the announcement. In some cases, you may be able to get the picture back for additional use or to frame.

Stationery Announcements

Don't order your engagement announcements from a bridal salon or bridal shop. Those establishments are targeted specifically toward the bridal consumer, and that usually means you'll be paying top dollar.

If you're ordering printed announcements of your engagement, shop around at stationery stores for the best prices. Look for special sales that can save you 10 percent, 20 percent, or more.

Order a simpler style of announcement. The price of a basic and very classy black print on white paper selection will go up if you choose a different typeface, color of print, or any additional graphics. Sometimes these savings can add up to 50 percent when you keep it simple.

Know exactly how many engagement announcements you'll need so you don't order too many. One bride spent fifty dollars—make that *wasted* fifty dollars—by ordering her announcements way before she'd reached a firm number of recipients. The extra announcements are sitting in a box in her closet.

❧

Simply buy some high-quality paper by the pound at a discount or stationery store and print your own announcements using a classy font on your home computer. An excellent designed paper source is Paper Direct (800-A-PAPERS; fax 201-507-0817). If you don't own a computer, use a friend's or one at the office.

❧

Either print the announcements up yourself, which is the least expensive way, or take a master copy to a discount print shop and have them do it for you. Whichever you choose, the cost will still be less than if you order name-brand announcements from a catalog or specialty store.

Store-ordered announcements	$50
Homemade announcements plus discount print shop	$25
Homemade plus home-copied announcements	$5

Perhaps the best news: If you're announcing the engagement at a party or gathering, you don't have to send out printed announcements at all. No one will miss them.

One Bride's Story:

> *For my announcements, I raided an after-Christmas 50-percent-off sale for holiday stationery. Then I printed up announcements using my home computer and the holiday stationery, and I mailed them out the day after Christmas. They turned out lovely and perfect for the season.*
>
> *—Frances, bride.*

2

Your Engagement Party

Because it's a less formal affair than the wedding itself, you'll find you can get away with providing most of the services for this party yourself.

Compare among store-bought engagement party invitations. The regular-sized ones are less expensive than the oversized ones, and the simpler ones are less expensive than the decorated ones with the shiny covers and the laser cutouts. Just be sure, though, that the invitation you choose will reflect the level of formality of the engagement party.

❧

If ordering your engagement party invitations from a printer, choose a simpler style. A plain white invitation with black ink rather than a baby blue one with navy ink will cost you less.

Make your own engagement party invitations on your home computer with a classy font and your own clip art for decoration. For further savings, search for quality paper for these homemade invitations. Your comparison shopping may find the best values at a buy-by-the-pound paper source. Again, check out Paper Direct (800-A-PAPERS).

Get your envelopes here, too. There's no need to spend extra for decorative, lined, or security envelopes.

Have the engagement party at home instead of at a reception hall or club. The comfortable, warm atmosphere is perfect for any level of formality.

If you're planning on having the engagement party catered, cut costs a bit by having only part of the meal prepared by the professionals. They make the entree, and you make the appetizers and desserts. You can easily cut a standard caterer's bill in half.

Or, for even bigger savings, don't have the engagement party catered. Instead, provide the food and drink yourself, and spend the day having fun in the kitchen with the groom and your bridal party. You'll spend much less per guest than you would have if you had hired a caterer to do the job, and the compliments you'll receive on the food will mean so much more.

Catered meal	$55 per guest
Home-prepared meal	$20–$30 per guest

Plan the engagement party for a time during the day when no meal will be expected. An informal affair from two to five is adequately served with hors d'oeuvres, and a soiree starting at seven is best served with cake and dessert.

Shop for food and supplies in bulk or at one of those discount supply houses. Have a friend take you on her membership if you don't belong to the club.

Cut down on beverage costs by serving nonalcoholic drinks. Punches stretch well, serving more people for the dollar. (Tip: Do what restaurants do and add lots of ice to each drink.)

Drinks Portion of Caterer's Bill

Events *with* alcohol $15–$20 more per person
Events *without* alcohol $10 more per person

200 guest list $3,000–$4,000 more for alcohol

Make your own cake, perhaps with a heart-shaped pan, or have a relative make the engagement party cake for you. Compare the price of a bakery-bought sheet cake with a few boxes of cake mix, ingredients, and icing, and you'll find huge savings here. If you're worried about the appearance of a homemade cake at your engagement party, follow the example of a wedding cake-making cookbook you'll find in the cooking section of your library. With some work, your creation may rival the professional's in beauty and taste.

Store-bought sheet cake	$45
Homemade sheet cake	$20

Take your own pictures, and pass around the camera for help from family and friends. You may hire a professional photographer to take pictures at your engagement party, but you're trying to save money here, not waste it. This is just the engagement party, so informal pictures will do fine.

Professional photographer	$700–$800
Do-it-yourself	$50
(includes price of film and developing)	

Instead of hiring a band, DJ, pianist, or harpist for your engagement party, turn on the stereo if the engagement party is being held in your home, or have the restaurant or reception hall pipe in appropriate music through its sound system.

| Professional music | $200–$300 |
| Stereo/piped-in music | free |

As for decorations, consider a simpler look. Fourteen dozen white balloons and curly streamers may look festive, but they're also a nonessential that can be thrown out in favor of saving some money. Instead, how about a computer-generated banner you made for free? Create a classier look by decorating with vases of flowers cut fresh from your garden.

Balloons and streamers	up to $75
Homemade banner	free
Vases of flowers from garden	free

Of course, you may choose not to have an engagement party at all. You could make your big announcement at a family gathering such as Thanksgiving dinner and save all the fanfare for the wedding itself.

3

Getting Organized

During the entire planning process, you'll have to keep track of thousands of details. Staying on top of approaching deadlines, ordering and pickup dates, and little but necessary specifics takes some work, but the effort means money saved and smoother progress.

Start planning and organizing early enough so that you have plenty of time to perform each job well. A rushed job means fewer chances to get more for your money. This may mean allowing more than a few months for the planning of your wedding and reception.

❧

If you want your own copy, encourage your mother or maid of honor to give you a wedding planner book as her gift to you. She'll feel a tug of sentimentality in the gesture, and you'll save some money at the bookstore. For discounted books and planners, check Barnes and Noble (800-242-6657).

Use your local library's supply of wedding etiquette books instead of buying your own. After all, when will you ever need a wedding etiquette book again?

Bookstore wedding books	$10–$20
Wedding book from library	free

Borrow a recently married relative's or friend's wedding etiquette books.

Set up an organizer file using four-by-six-inch index cards and a recipe card file box. You've seen this suggested in all your bridal magazines and even in some ads for fifty-dollar index card and file box sets with printed labels. Setting up a wedding planner file box of your own will work just as well, if not better.

You could also choose to turn an accordion file into your wedding organizer system. You'll find these in any office supply store for just a few dollars. Label each slot with subject headings—Gown, Flowers, Music, Caterer—and filing brochures and swatches is simple.

Use your organization system to keep track of receipts, brochures, pictures, drawings, business cards, and all the important things that can get lost in your car or office. The rule goes: If you've lost it now, you'll need it later. And that can cost you money if something needs to be returned or an order needs to be placed.

As you've seen here, you can set up your own organization system for pennies. Besides the fact that it's customized to your tastes and needs, it's a huge savings compared with the cost of one of those computer wedding-planner programs. Do you really need your IBM to remind you to go for your fitting at four o'clock? Besides, you can't file your brochures, swatches, and store receipts in the computer's "files." While going high tech is a fun idea, it's also one of the worst cases of unnecessary wedding spending you'll ever see. Skip the software and stick with your own files, folders, or binder.

All right, all right. If you really, really, really want to use one of those new wedding planner software packages on your home computer, there are inexpensive ways to go about it. Either put it on your gift wish list (organization-crazy mothers of the bride always seem to take the bait), or round up your three other engaged girlfriends so you can all share it. This might mean passing the disk down the line after each one of you is finished with it, and that's not necessarily the best arrangement available, but it's a way to cut your costs a little. Here are a few on the market:

An Enchanted Wedding
(Windows) $59.95 + $4 postage
(Macintosh)   69.95 + $4 postage
Enchanted Software   (800-255-3683)

Bridesmaid
(Windows) $54.95 + $4.50 postage
Simply Software   (800-425-1122)

Wedding Workshop
(Windows or Macintosh)   call for price
MicroProcision Software   (800-688-9337)

Egghead Software (800-344-4323)
Selective Software (800-423-3556)

Or you could just set up files on your home computer without a fancy software package—a free option in place of an expensive one.

What about those fifty-dollar video wedding planners? Most brides say those tapes contain little more than the average wedding planner found in the library, plus a lot of scanning of wedding sites and models in gowns. The brides' advice? Skip it, rent it on dollar day at your rental store, or watch the copy the library owns.

Always make absolutely sure that your decisions are final before you contract for services and items. This includes, of course, running your plans by the groom and by those who are helping to finance the wedding. A hastily made decision means money lost when a contract has to be canceled or an item returned.

Get everything in writing. Written records can be referred to easily for reminders and deadlines, and oral contracts will not hold up in court in case of a problem. A written record of any business agreement should include these details for clarification: the date of sale, the business's name and phone number, your own name and phone number, date of service, time of service, location of service, details of the service or items, delivery arrangements, payment arrangements, check number, cancellation or postponement policy, refund policy, and the name and signature of the person who took the order. Also, always get a copy of any contract and confirmation numbers from the professionals who will be providing services during your ceremony or reception.

Read every word of your contracts, even if you have to sit back in your chair while the impatient salesclerk rolls his eyes and tries to hurry you along to the check-writing stage. You never know what's hidden in the fine print—extra charges, commissions, outlandish gratuities, conditions, waivers, etc.

If you don't understand something in the contract, don't hesitate to ask. If the clerk is throwing business jargon at you, ask for clarification.

Just to be on the safe side, photocopy your contracts and keep the copies in a secure place. In case of loss, theft, or fire, you're still on secure ground with the larger expenses of your wedding.

Get receipts for each of your deposits, signed and dated by the salesclerk. This way, you're preventing the old you-never-paid-me trick some shadier companies might try on you.

If you do wind up with a problem, go straight to the manager. No boss wants his or her business to get a bad report made by an unhappy customer. Wedding industry professionals know that much of their business comes from referrals, and a bad reputation can slow down the flow of customers. The manager, you'll find, will be quick to fix the problems. If not, go to consumer action groups and consumer action columns in your local paper (that'll get them hopping to please you), the Better Business Bureau if you fear for those who will come along after you, and the professional association affiliated with the business itself. Check your Yellow Pages for your state's agencies.

Keep lists so you don't forget anything. Follow the lists provided in wedding books and magazines, or make up your own. (Ask the groom, the bridal party, and your families to do the same.)

Keep several pads and pencils around the house, in your car, and at the office for when a thought or a question strikes you. Another rule of the wedding planner: If you think you'll remember it later, you won't. Write it down.

Keep a mini tape recorder, if you have one, in your purse or car for the same reason.

One of your most important lists should be a price comparison list. Accounting ledgers are good for this job. You'll be able to assign each caterer, photographer, or band its own column, where you'll record prices and package details. Use this setup as you price all the services you'll need. A quick glance down a column on one piece of paper will reveal the choice with the best price and the most attractive offerings for that price. One bride who used this system found that she was better able to compare all the different packages and in picking the best one saved herself three hundred fifty dollars.

Keep a master list of phone numbers so you don't have to keep looking up important numbers or calling information. Each call to your phone company's directory number can cost you several dollars.

Record upcoming deadlines on both your home and work calendars, and record there what you've already done as well. You may need to know exactly what day you ordered your gown so the salesperson can tell you if yours has arrived in the latest shipment.

For each service you're arranging, call to confirm your order, delivery, and prices several times throughout the wedding planning months. You never can be too sure.

> *It was a good thing I called to confirm. The florist said she had lost her appointment book in a robbery, and she had no idea which weddings were planned for which days. She said it was lucky I called her. That's an understatement.*
>
> *—Stacy, bride.*

Send confirmation letters, and keep copies for yourself both as proof and as reminders of each step in the process.

Keep samples of fabric, ribbon, and lace and pictures of your gown and reception site in a box in your car so that you'll always have access to them when you're out shopping, at a big fabric sale, or in another city. Never guess at the color of your bridesmaids' dresses when you're out to buy coordinating items. A clash is a waste of money and shows your guests that you were unorganized and trying too hard to save some money.

Keep track of every wedding response you receive. Your final head count depends on those numbers, and it is that figure that tallies up one of the biggest expenses of your wedding: the catering. Keep your responses and a working Yay and Nay list in a large envelope or in your organizer bound with a rubber band.

Do you really need a wedding coordinator to keep you organized? Some women swear by their services, claiming that the organizer was responsible for putting together a wedding that couldn't possibly have been more perfect. While it's important to recognize the value of a coordinator to someone who has no time to plan the wedding or is too distant from where the wedding will be held—cases in which hiring an organizer can actually save money—it's also a money-saving fact that you can do the job of a wedding coordinator yourself. It takes time and a lot of footwork, but most brides say that's the best part of planning the wedding. Handing those jobs over to a stranger—and paying hundreds if not thousands of dollars for it—just may not make sense to you.

Or hire the most efficient and least expensive wedding consultant ever known—your mother. After all, consider her feelings. She may feel left out of the experience and honor of planning her daughter's wedding.

If you *need* a wedding consultant—either because you're much too busy to call thirty bakeries for prices or because you're several states away from where the wedding will be held—be sure the consultant you choose is a good one. Ask for references.

Ask a recently married friend if she'd recommend the consultant she used.

Make sure the consultant is a member of the Association of Bridal Consultants (203-355-0464). Considering how much you'll be paying, it's best to make sure the person you hire is legitimate and well trained.

When you hire a wedding consultant, carefully review the guidelines set up for your business relationship. Make sure you're both clear where your responsibilities begin and end, and don't hesitate to ask questions. It's *your* wedding.

A common situation facing more and more brides today is the problem of distance. Maybe it's because we're traveling more, meeting our men in places that bring people from distant parts together, and our faxes and computers make it easier to carry on serious long-distance relationships. Whatever the reason, you'll still have to keep in contact with both his and your family and friends miles away during the planning stages of the wedding. Long-distance communication can cost money—a whole lot of it—so follow these steps for better, more economical distance organization:

Calling on the phone can be expensive if your bridal party, family, and even the groom live out of town, so pick up the receiver only if it's really important.

Know your phone company's off-rate hours and call then to save money on each call. At economy rates, the price per minute for your call could be half the regular rate. That translates into cutting your phone bills by 50 percent, and some brides have saved themselves up to two hundred dollars.

Send letters regularly, updating on changes and decisions, asking for help or advice, and thanking everyone for their cooperation up to that point. The price here: a mere twenty-nine cents per letter.

Use postcards for short messages such as arrival dates, rehearsal times, fitting dates, etc.

Fax them a letter for less than a phone call, or . . .

Send a message via your computer's modem. Just check out the expense first to be sure you're not sacrificing price for speed.

Instead of mailing several pages out of a bridal magazine or the magazine itself, just tell your bridesmaids what issue and page they should see. They then can go to their library or bookstore to see the dress or shoes or hairstyle themselves.

Send a copy of the wedding schedule to each member of the bridal party, the families, and friends who will be taking part in the wedding in other ways. This way, everyone is sure about what days to keep clear way in advance. Dates and times will not have to be shuffled.

Have the bridesmaids, honor attendants, best man, and ushers send you their measurements and sizes on index cards. With this information, you won't have to phone around to get them to admit their sizes when it's time to order their apparel. If shyness is a problem, have them send you their index cards in sealed envelopes to be opened only by the salesperson at the shop.

Important: Tell your attendants to have their sizes measured at a professional tailor's or seamstress's workshop; measurements taken with a tape measure or a piece of string and a ruler aren't nearly as legitimate. One bridesmaid who took her own measurements with a tape measure misread her hip measurement and ordered the wrong size dress. When it arrived, it didn't fit, and she had to buy another dress on the double.

To help your attendants and your families to stay organized—and to keep them from calling you all the time for one another's phone numbers—send out phone and address lists of all the key players.

Keep everyone up to date on all the plans that have been made. This includes your families, the bridal party, the parents of child attendants, and those who will be taking part in the ceremony as readers, performers, or guest registrars.

If a bridal party or family member is slow in responding with important information, don't hesitate to explain how important it is to stay with the schedule. Apply some gentle pressure to get the job done. Or just use the broken record approach. Call the person up and say, "I don't remember if I've already asked you this, but did you send me your size card already?" Of course you know she didn't, but it doesn't hurt to play forgetful if your point gets across.

4

Finding Savings at Bridal Shows

The bridal show is a staged event to get the bride in a spending mood. It's all advertising, all glitz, and all fun. Countless brides and their bridal parties and mothers show up at bridal shows in salons and malls every weekend to learn what the pros say are the biggest, best, and hottest styles and ideas for today's wedding. It may not sound like the bridal show is the place to be when you're trying to save some money, but it does have redeeming qualities.

❧

Go to the bridal show to collect brochures, business cards, and prices (if they're available at the show) for your research. No need to travel all over town to all the bridal shops, shoe stores, caterers, florists, and photographers if each has information set up and available at the bridal show.

Just use the show to get a sense of what you want in a three-dimensional representation of what you'd see in a bridal magazine.

Look at everything at the bridal show in terms of "How can I make this?"—especially decorations and favors.

Some businesses set up at the bridal show may offer discounts to those brides who sign up for their services on the spot. This takes away from your ability to comparison shop, so it may not be a good idea to go for the offer right away. Take time to check before you commit. You can always come back if the show will be running through the weekend.

Door prizes are awarded at most bridal shows. They can range from silver frames to gift certificates for a wedding-day makeover. Any gift is money in your pocket.

Speaking of gifts, you'll find samples of every kind at bridal shows. Makeup, perfumes, little portions of cake—all offered there for you to try without expense or obligations. So take advantage.

While you're there, see if there are any mailing lists you'd like to get on. Perhaps you'll be offered discounts. Just be prepared later for an onslaught of mail. The list you sign and the information you give may be sold to other retailers and businesses looking to attract your checkbook. For information on dates and times for bridal shows scheduled for your area, call 800-422-3976 for the Great Bridal Expo; Macy's stores across the nation hold regular bridal events.

5

Your Bridal Registry

Registering for your wedding gifts is the fun part. You get to shop for everything you could possibly want without having to spend a dime. OK, so you don't get to take the goods home with you right away, but it's exciting to know that you'll eventually wind up with some of the items you've chosen. Bring the groom along and let him be in charge of the pen and clipboard. Include him as much as possible in decisions that will affect his life, too.

Meet with the bridal registry consultant before you begin filling out your choices. She'll be able to answer your questions, direct you to resources you wouldn't have known about otherwise, and tell you about special messages and directions you can add to your registry file. Karen and Greg added this message to their registry file: "We prefer simple and elegant styles rather than busy or patterned styles." They received all appropriate items and saved themselves the hassle and expense of exchanges.

Obviously, it's smarter to register for things you need—like blankets, a coffee maker, a microwave oven—than to fill your dream sheet with all those fun little extras and gadgets such as a shampoo dispenser for the shower or a personalized doormat. The idea is for the guests to help you set up your household, not to fill it with junk you'll have to clear out of the way for the new microwave you had to buy with your wedding money.

If you're going to register for things you need, why not register at a place other than the local china and crystal store? Home Depot has a popular registry system set up, and many brides and grooms are finding it much more to their liking to receive tools and household appliances they really need. Look up the nearest Home Depot in your phone book. The following catalogs and companies also offer registry services:

L. L. Bean	800-341-4341
Barron's	800-538-6340
Crate and Barrel	800-323-5461
Tiffany & Co.	800-323-3661
Williams Sonoma	800-541-2233

Let your friends and family know by word of mouth where you're registered so that you know you'll be getting exactly what you wanted. (It's considered rude to print your registry information in a party invitation.)

Be sure to have your address printed at the top of the registry file so that guests who are unable to attend your wedding will know where to send their gifts.

When you're writing down which toaster, wok, and pressure cooker you'd like, be sure to write down the model numbers of the items, so that you will receive exactly what you want.

If the registry form doesn't have a space for them, enter the color themes of each room of your house in the "extras" section. That way, you'll be eliminating the problem of "Nice quilt, but it clashes with our colors."

After you hand in your registry checklist, plan to get a printout of your registry as soon as it's entered into the computer. Search for and correct mistakes in your file right away.

Plan to update your registry after each wave of gifts arrives—from your engagement party, showers, your own shopping trips throughout the months of planning—to prevent your receiving duplicates.

After your wedding, get a printout of your registry so you'll have a record of the things you wanted but didn't receive. It's a ready-made birthday, anniversary, and Christmas gift list.

6

Your Bridal Party

Choose a smaller bridal party, perhaps limited to sisters and brothers. After all, if you have eight bridesmaids and eight ushers plus flower girls and ring bearers, you'll have to pay for that many gifts, perhaps arrange lodging for all of them, rent more limos, etc. Not only is a smaller bridal party a savings for you, it will also prevent headaches over which of your cousins, friends, and coworkers to include in the lineup. One bride estimated her expenses per attendant—including gifts, planning luncheons, and apparel (her choice)—to be one hundred seventy-five dollars. Others estimated their per-attendant amount in the fifty-to-seventy-five dollar range.

Consider just having a maid or matron of honor and a best man as your bridal party. Male relatives can act as ushers purely to seat the guests.

Just have flower girls. It's a charming look. Beverly, a bride, was able to outfit and buy gifts for her six flower-girls for the cost of one designer-style bridesmaid's dress.

Rather than having to choose a few friends out of a handful of special ones, choose none. The same goes for your twelve first cousins.

When you choose your bridal party, particularly the maid or matron of honor and best man, be sure you can depend on the people you're involving. Maturity and dependability are important. You don't want to include disinterested people who aren't able to keep appointments and deadlines because a big party just came up or something really good was on television. Remember, your bridal party is more than just a collection of well-dressed men and women; the position has meaning and purpose. You don't want to have to spend your time and money backtracking on the responsibilities of your attendants.

Don't be pressured to choose people based on their standing in the family in general (such as all cousins). Your honor attendants should be individually special to you.

Don't include obviously bitter, jealous, or unsupportive attendants or ushers out of a sense of responsibility. These people will be impossible to work with, and they'll put a damper on your day.

Don't include someone just because you were in her bridal party years ago. You should *not* use your wedding to "pay back" people.

The best way to save money on your bridal party is to keep them updated on your decisions, to supply them with lists of their responsibilities and deadlines, and to be receptive to their input throughout. People management is a smart way to save yourself extra trouble and expense.

7

Setting a Budget

The best way to control your spending is to follow a budget. Temptation spending is less of a threat when you have a general outline to follow. Several factors will control your budget, and you may find it harder to control some more than others. Where you live, for instance, will affect the prices of services available to you, and there's not much you can realistically do about that. On the other hand, your guest list and the formality of your wedding are major factors. With some creative management of these, your budget will be more manageable.

Before you sit down to create your wedding budget, research the prices of basic wedding services in your area. That way, your budget will be more realistic.

List every single expense you will have to face. Start with the obvious ones, then look through magazines and ask married friends about all those hidden extras. To cheer yourself up, list what you can get for free.

Then make another list of the top three or four things on which you'll spare no expense—or at least not scrimp too much on. These may be your gown, the catering, your honeymoon—whatever you feel most strongly about. With these items arranged, you'll be better able to find the right places to cut spending.

Add to your list of expenses a reserve for any miscellaneous spending that may come up, such as taxes, tips, and transport fees, so you're not chipping away at the main budget with all the little things.

Look at your available cash flow to see where you stand. Designate a percentage of your savings and projected income until the wedding date to determine your wedding funds. You don't want to throw yourself far into debt with loans or a drain on your credit cards, and you don't want to sell your prized possessions to dig yourself out of the hole after the big day. Don't plan to spend the amount you expect in wedding checks. It's better to stick with what you have than to overextend yourselves.

Decide how the expenses will be divided. What will your parents be able and willing to finance? The groom's parents? What will you foot the bill for yourselves? This list will take some work, as money can be a highly sensitive issue to everyone involved in planning a wedding. Foster a sense of cooperation and compromise. Full input by all is recommended so that no one feels as if they've been unfairly assigned an expenditure. The result will be a smart outline for the handling of your wedding budget.

Try to save money for everyone involved. Bear in mind your families' and friends' cash flow when you make decisions that will affect them, and they in turn will try to help save money for you as well.

Be sensitive if one family is in a higher income bracket than the other. It's unfair to burden one with the job of keeping up with the other. Keep expenses for both groups even so neither family feels they're doing more than the other. Nothing fosters family tensions faster than money problems.

Don't push expenses off onto your families. Not only is it inconsiderate to ask too much, you could be handing over a certain amount of control over your decisions as well. What bride hasn't heard, "I'm paying for this, aren't I?"

Keep a working record of your expenses as you go along. It's best to keep on top of the flow of checks and bills.

Don't become a slave to the magic number. Your budget is just a framework to keep your spending under control. If the flowers actually cost you sixty-five dollars more than you'd expected, don't cut the grandmothers' corsages just to slide under the limit. Most brides believe they lost control of their spending (not to mention their temper) to a greater degree when they felt most bogged down by the budget they'd arranged months ago.

If you think the budget might turn into additional pressure for you (perhaps you've had experience with budgeting before), set your limits slightly higher than you'd like them to be. An extra ten dollars tacked onto each projected expenditure could make you feel triumphant instead of guilty when you sign the photographer's contract for five dollars under your budget. (I know it's a game you play on yourself, but it's important to downplay the significance of the money so that you don't start to feel it's controlling your wedding.)

If you do arrange a service for well below the amount you originally budgeted for it, exercise great control by not blowing the amount you saved on something trivial. Instead, enter that amount in a reserve that will allow you to slip slightly over budget in another category . . . like your gown.

Lower the number of guests if you need to cut expenses. Just don't try this after the invitations have been sent. You can't uninvite a person.

Lower the formality of the wedding if your introductory research shows that a formal dinner reception will be just too expensive. Choose a more economical alternative, such as a luncheon or a tea party.

Caterer's Prices

Full dinner for fifty	$55 per guest
Luncheon for fifty	$30 per guest
Tea party for fifty	$20 per guest

Another way to cut down the budget is to ask friends and relatives how they might be able to help you out. Borrowing and free services are the best ways to save money on your wedding.

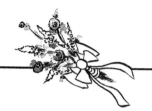

8

The Season and Date
of Your Wedding

Believe it or not, a wedding held today may be twice as expensive as an identical wedding held six months from now . . . or half the price. It all depends on the season. Holidays, the weather, and tourism all affect the prices and availability of services you may want to reserve for your wedding. Ask about seasonal price changes when you're pursuing general information from the professionals listed below.

First, allow yourself plenty of time to consider several seasons for your wedding. This might mean up to a year of waiting and planning, but you can save a lot of money with careful research in this area.

Ask about seasonal charges for the ceremony location. More popular wedding months may see a rise in location fees.

Ask about seasonal charges for the reception location as well. Again, busier wedding months may mean the manager has boosted—or dropped—package rates.

The season of your wedding also determines if you'll have weather factors to consider. Are you planning an outdoor wedding during the rainy season? If so, the garden tea party you found to be so much less expensive than the sit-down dinner will wind up costing you much more than you had planned when you have to move everyone and everything indoors. What about the air conditioning or heat you'll have to provide?

Will it be the stormy time of year where you're planning to spend your honeymoon? A great deal of money is wasted if you lose a day or two of your vacation because a flight was delayed by a hurricane. So consider the seasonal weather when you plan your wedding and honeymoon.

The travel industry is also controlled by seasonal rates. Off-season airfare and hotel reservations can amount to hundreds of dollars' savings over high-season tourist prices. Check with your travel agent about seasonal travel prices when you begin your planning, or check directly with airlines and hotels.

Holidays also affect the price of travel for the bride and groom and for family and friends who will come from miles away to share your day with you. Either travel and lodging fees will soar skyward due to holiday visiting, or special holiday travel packages may be offered to lure passengers away from competitors. Research holiday travel rates thoroughly before you plunk down a few thousand on Memorial Day weekend. You might be able to get a better deal at another time.

Another way to facilitate travel: plan your wedding for the weekend of a family gathering or reunion. Everyone will be in the general area, and they'll get two great events for one trip. One bride found that when she moved her wedding date to an earlier weekend, more of her guests would be in the area after a family party, and she saved over a thousand dollars in travel and lodging for her guests.

The season of your wedding will also affect the price of the flowers you choose for your bouquets and decorations. Blooms and plants are usually cheaper when they're in season, so consider your florist bill when you set a date on the calendar. Furthermore, a wedding planned for Valentine's Day faces an increased charge for much-in-demand roses. Sixty-dollar bouquets on Valentine's Day go for less than twenty dollars the day after, so imagine what your wedding flowers will cost.

Prices and types of food on the wedding menu will also be affected by the season. Warmer days mean lighter, simpler foods, and certain types of seafood are less expensive when in season.

Which months are the best to consider? It's hard to say. May through August are the busiest, and high demand usually means inflated prices and slimmer choices. December, too, is a popular month for weddings, and, due to the high prices of the holiday season, it's also costly. Spring break may see a fare hike on airlines. Graduation time may mean caterers and entertainers are busy with those celebrations. So what's left? January through April and September to November. Be careful, though. These may be the natural down time for the wedding industry, but there's no guarantee that rates will be better than at the busiest times. In fact, depending on where you are and what kind of wedding season preceded the down time, prices just might be higher. Research is key.

A Saturday wedding in your area may cost less than a Sunday wedding. If airlines can charge different prices for popular days of travel, so can reception halls. The date of the wedding really can make a difference in the money you'll spend. The only way to beat the system is to do your homework and research seasonal shifts in prices.

9

The Time of Day

For their own reasons, some wedding sites charge different rates for different times of the day, so it may be less expensive to have the ceremony in the morning than in the afternoon or evening. When researching ceremony locations, look through price brochures or ask questions to find out if your choice has a time factor in the fees.

According to wedding tradition and etiquette standards, the time of day of the wedding and reception determines the degree of formality. A morning wedding and brunch will cost nowhere near the total for the ultraformal candlelight ceremony and eight o'clock sit-down dinner affair. So when choosing a time to reserve the ceremony site and reception hall, consider the festivities appropriate to that time of day.

Beyond formality, it's just less expensive to serve your guests a range of hors d'oeuvres at one in the afternoon than filet mignon at nine in the evening. Plan your menu according to time of day for greater savings. Done properly, offering hors d'oeuvres can be every bit as classy as the full-meal arrangement. More so, perhaps, depending on your choices and presentation.

Another plus for the earlier reception: it's easier to get away with having an economical nonalcoholic reception earlier in the afternoon than it is at night.

An earlier ceremony and reception also means you'll have plenty of time in the evening to set off on your honeymoon. You'll save money this way by not having to pay seventy-five dollars for a post-reception hotel room the night before an early flight.

10

Your Wedding Location

Of course, your church or synagogue may be the obvious choice for reasons other than the minimal expense of reserving it for your ceremony. Most establishments just ask for a donation and an officiant's fee, and that is still much better than a five-hundred-dollar location rental bill.

Meet with your officiant about scheduling and restrictions. You'll need to know before you make any plans or put down any deposits if there are rules about which musical selections and performers you can arrange and whether photographers are allowed. If, for instance, you find that your church does not allow harp music during wedding ceremonies, you will lose the deposit you already gave to the harpist.

Be up-front about any special information the officiant should know. Attempting to hide such things as your different religions is a very bad idea. You could find your ceremony canceled on you if your officiant is strict about limits.

Your Search for a Wedding Location

Look around far in advance.

Use a place with which you are familiar.

Make sure the location is suitable for your religions.

Make sure the location is suitable for the number of guests who will be attending your ceremony.

Make sure the location offers the necessary facilities: restrooms, electricity, parking, handicapped access. . . .

Will it be necessary to rent chairs and other items in order to use this location for the ceremony? It could turn out to be an expensive proposition, as chair rentals can reach into the hundreds of dollars.

Make sure you will be allowed enough time in that location for the completion of your ceremony. You don't want to be rushed out of the place so the next wedding can begin.

Does this location match the formality of your wedding?

Will your deposit be returned if you decide against this location?

If it is an outdoor setting you're considering, be sure to add in the weather factor. You may have to move if it begins to rain. And if you miss the rainstorm, you'll still have mud to contend with.

Some economical settings to rent for your ceremony: restaurant, service-club hall, gallery, social or country club, community center.

While some licensed wedding sites charge you a fee up front to use their property, other equally breathtaking locations are free for the asking. Here are a few places to look:

Have your wedding at a mansion. Check with your local historical society for details, and you'll find a variety of gorgeous homes with some historical significance open to you as a setting for your day. Either hold the festivities indoors, perhaps in the grand dining room, or make use of the mansion's garden and gazebo.

Check with your local historical society for other ideas for free wedding locations. They may be able to direct you to a wonderful and noteworthy spot you'll love.

Consider a winery for an intimate gathering. Many brides find this to be a location more suited to their personality—and pocketbook—than a full-blown extravaganza fit for royalty.

Consider your college or military chapel or banquet hall. As an alumnus or a veteran, you may have access for a limited charge. For instance, the U.S. Naval Academy in Annapolis, Maryland, is a favorite wedding location for Annapolis graduates and members of the Navy and Marines, among others.

A banquet hall at work will do. Check your place of business, your groom's, your families', your friends'.

A wedding held at home may be enticing as a free location, but remember to add on the cost of decorations and the rental of tables and other necessities. Be sure you won't end up paying more than you would for a modest reception hall location.

Perhaps a friend or relative could offer as their wedding gift to you the use of their yacht or nearby vacation home. Those close to you with resources will undoubtedly be honored that you'd even consider their place for your wedding.

How about a wedding held at a scenic overlook? You'll notice that many fancy reception halls have large picture windows overlooking a glittering city skyline, an inspiring sunset over the water, a blooming valley. To enjoy the same backdrop, you don't have to book a room at three hundred dollars a head; just search for an area with a splendid scenic overlook and make the necessary arrangements with your town to hold your wedding there.

A wedding on the beach is still one of the most romantic choices available to you. For the nominal price of an official license to gather in the oceanside spot you choose and various permissions that are more legwork than check-work, you have available to you a priceless wedding location.

Other options: try a park, or a lake, or a beautiful garden.

Another inexpensive setting more suitable to the informal or semiformal wedding is a field of flowers. Nothing approaches the beauty of nature more closely than the beauty of matrimony. Again, though, all that beauty may still require a license from your town. Drinking in public and gathering after dark may be against the public order in some regions. A quick check can save you a fortune in tickets.

Don't take a standby position on a location schedule just because it's cheaper. There's too much invested in this wedding for you to depend on a maybe for the most important part of the day.

The Reception Hall

Look back at the previous chapter. Many of the same questions, concerns, and ideas will apply here.

If you've chosen to have your reception at a reception hall, avoid the top-of-the-line places with the largest ads in the newspaper and the celebrity clientele. Their prices will be inflated by their status as a prime wedding location, and they can sometimes be too gaudy for the average person's tastes. Instead, compare all the choices available to you very carefully. Look at the entire package, not just the pretty scenery.

Choose a reception location that already has tables and chairs and equipment so you don't have to rent those separately. Of course, the price for this place may be higher, but you have to add in the value of the items you're not having to rent.

When you're checking out reception halls, consider these points: Is the place clean? How many waiters or servers will be working your reception? How many other receptions will be going on at the same time as yours? Are the walls soundproof enough to keep out the sounds of the other receptions? Search out all the details that you think could possibly affect your reception, and question the manager about them.

Comparison shop between reception locations, and keep track of these places on graph paper so you can check off what each hall offers for its price. Leave space for your own notes about each place as well.

Consider a smaller, more intimate banquet hall or room for your reception. You may need to trim your guest list slightly, but the price per person is bound to be much lower than the too-large rooms that drip with crystal and glare with fancy lighting.

If your family has a favorite restaurant that you've been going to for years, you obviously already trust its dependability. So don't rule out their reception services just because it's not a new place. Most brides enjoy not having to worry whether or not the food will be good. One bride even received a 33 percent-off credit for her wedding at a favorite restaurant's banquet room, just because she and her family had been loyal customers for years.

An outdoor setting means added cost for rentals, the arrangement of facilities, and more. When you add it all up, make sure you're getting the best deal.

If you're planning an outdoor reception, plan an alternate setting in case it rains. To be doubly sure, map out instructions for a quick move in case the skies break with little time to set up in a new place. Having to hold the wedding on a rain date can mean extra expenses and some lost services with no refunds, so it's smart to have a same-day plan.

The arboretum, winery, mansion, or beach setting you arranged for your ceremony will work just as beautifully for your reception. Besides, having a setting work double duty for you means you won't have to worry about transportation from the ceremony to the reception. That could mean a total of five hundred dollars or more in your pocket. See how savings just pile up when you're looking for them?

One last reception setting option: You can transform a social association's multipurpose party room or a church hall into a pretty locale for your celebration. It may take some extra yards of material, a creative team, and some work, but it can be done nicely. Some organizations even can spruce up the place for you for a small donation to their cause.

The reception location you choose may require you to rent such items as tables, chairs, china, chafing dishes, and linens. Save money in this arena by following these tips:

Look at the items you're arranging to rent before you commit to them. The china may be hideous, and the glasses chipped.

Carefully review all items when they are delivered, noting broken or marred pieces in order to prevent your having to pay damages. Have the delivery person record the damages and sign this record. Several months ago, a bride didn't get this proof, and the company made her replace twenty chipped wine goblets.

Have the items cleaned afterward, if those are the terms of your contract, and ready to be returned on time. A delay may mean extra charges.

Simply use your own china and glassware if you have enough of a similar style to go around or borrow from friends and relatives.

 *12*

Religious Elements

Ask your officiant for a copy of the guidelines and restrictions of your church or synagogue. Ask questions to clarify. Certain things may not be allowed in your ceremony—such as a unity candle or a secular song performed by a professional singer—and it's best to find out before you spend money on them.

If you find it necessary to do some research on the religious elements of your ceremony or reception, skip the seventy-five-dollar religious advisor's fee and talk directly to the wedding officiant.

Look up the customs of your faith in books and articles free in your public library, or borrow a religious wedding guidebook from a friend or relative.

If you need special ceremonial items, such as a satin ring-bearer's pillow, a white aisle runner, a unity candle, or a chuppah, make or borrow them if you can. Or see if your church or synagogue will allow you to borrow theirs. Mandy, a recent bride, regrets not having done this. Her florist charged her one hundred twenty-five dollars for an aisle runner that looked like a giant paper towel roll.

Don't plan to add on to any religious ritual or practice unless you've talked to the officiant about it. Most officiants have their own rules, and these must not be crossed or altered without permission.

By all means include readings and a performance of music in your religious ceremony. Perhaps reading a religious passage, playing an instrument, or singing a hymn could be a relative's or a friend's gift to you.

13

Your Gown

Without a doubt your wedding gown will be a central focus of your budget. After all, the wedding gown is what most people think of when they think of a wedding. It's what will set you apart on your day. So this is one area where you don't want to go to extremes to save money. Smart shopping is one thing; inviting disaster with a too-good-to-be-true price on a possible fake from an overpriced bridal salon is another. So here are some smart money tips for getting the perfect wedding gown for you.

Start looking right away. Give yourself plenty of time to search out the perfect gown.

Don't order the gown before you have a date set for the wedding. If you order a summer gown and your wedding, it turns out, will have to be held in the winter, you'll lose money when you have to cancel your gown and reorder another.

Never order a dress you haven't seen. You could get stuck with something that doesn't match a sketch or description. And you might not get your money back. (Some catalog gowns do have clear return policies.)

Avoid the big, fancy salons. You may think they're a great source of everything you need, and to some they may be, but you're also unlikely to get the best prices there. Salons are expensive (how else do you think they pay for all those lights, the plush pink carpeting, and the free cappuccino?), and an aggressive salesperson may pressure you into spending more money than you'd planned. After all, if she works on commission, she gets a bigger cut of whatever you wind up paying. On top of the gown, you may also pay high prices for alterations. So just to be safe and to give yourself a better chance to save money, skip the neon bridal salons.

Call or send a letter to find out about prices and ordering information. You may even learn that the particular gown you like is being discontinued and therefore offered at a special discount price. One bride found her dream gown this way. She learned it was on the discontinued list, ordered up one of the remaining ones in the company's stock, and saved two hundred dollars.

Some gown ads also list the stores and chains where you can find the gown you like. Use the company's list of stores, if you can get to the cities they mention, for your dress hunting so you're confident that you're not buying a copy of a designed gown.

Look through bridal magazines and catalogs to get an idea of what you really like. If you've purchased the magazine or received it as a gift, tear out the pages of the gowns you like and keep them together as possibilities. If you've borrowed the magazine from the library, just mark the pages with a paper clip and bring it along to the stores.

In those magazines, you'll find toll-free numbers and addresses you can use to get more information about the wedding gowns you like. Listed below are several catalogs that offer good values. Send for brochures and more information by calling the toll-free numbers:

Advantage Bridal Wear Stores	818-282-9206
Alfredo Angelo	1075 Broken Sound Parkway
	Boca Raton FL 33487
Amsale	800-765-0170
Bridal Originals	800-876-GOWN
Country Elegance	212-302-5906
Discount Bridal Service	800-874-8794
Eden	818-441-8715
Fink	212-921-5683
Galina Bouquet	212-564-1020
Impression	800-BRIDAL1
Jasmine	708-519-7778
Jessica McClintock	800-333-5301
Joelle	212-736-8811
Laura Ashley	800-223-6917
Lili	818-282-4326
Moonlight	708-884-7199
Venus	800-OHVENUS

So where should you look if not in the big bridal salons? Start in smaller bridal salons. You'll find them in the Yellow Pages or in ads in your local newspaper. They need to make less profit on each gown because they don't have to worry about upkeep on their marble floors and chandeliers. Of course, by opting away from the big salon you're sacrificing the posh, first-class service, but if you're determined to save money on nonessentials you'll find the smaller stores offer just as much of what you really need.

> *I had one gown in mind—and I didn't want any gown but that one. I checked in the big stores and in the catalogs, but no go. I guess it was too simple and classic a style for them to keep in stock. And then one day on a whim I walked into a quaint little bridal store that was no bigger than my kitchen, and there it was! The one gown I wanted, just hanging there like it was waiting for me. The woman behind the counter was so nice, she even suggested an outstanding seamstress whose prices were lowest in the area. I was so pleased, I ordered my bridesmaids' gowns from there too.*
>
> *—Shea, bride.*

If you're able to, look at bridal stores in different parts of your city, different cities, even different states. In a "richer" area, you're likely to find that prices are higher because the clientele can afford the amount asked. In more middle-class areas, prices are a bit lower. You may be able to find your dream dress across town for a hundred dollars less. Or your cousin in Delaware may find the dress for much less than its New York price tag.

When you're searching for a gown in several bridal shops, comparison shop like crazy. Take note of each store's policy on alterations, ordering time, refund rules, and flexibility. Check the quality of their work. Is the on-site seamstress frazzled and looking way behind schedule? Is the stock in good condition and relatively new? What kinds of guarantees can they give you? It pays to put in the time to compare the places that might outfit you on your wedding day. You'll want the best quality service your budget can buy. One bride used a notebook to record facts, figures, and observations about each bridal shop she considered. Her research paid off well—the shop she chose ended up saving her two hundred dollars more than the others would have.

If you have a friend or relative who works in a dress shop or a department store, see if she'll let you use her employee's discount. Ten to twenty percent off a five-hundred-dollar gown is a savings of fifty to a hundred dollars.

Look in the bridal sections of major department stores. While business there may have been crowded out in the past by fancy salons, brides today are coming back to the basics in gown shopping. They're looking for quality and a good price again, so the glitz of a salon may not be their first choice anymore.

When narrowing down choices, check with your state's Better Business Bureau to see if the companies are clear. Have there been any complaints or reports against them? At worst, are they operating illegally? We've all heard the horror stories about the dress shops that mysteriously disappeared in the middle of the night, leaving hundreds of brides without their gowns and the thousands of dollars they paid for them the week before the wedding. Unfortunately, it has happened and it could happen again. So consult the reporting agency to see if your store is legitimate and free of suspicious record. When you're dealing with something as important as your gown, it's best to protect yourself from all angles.

Be sure the gown you choose fits the level of formality of your wedding. You won't wear an ultraformal gown with a ten-foot train to a tea party in the garden. Staying within your level of formality will keep you from spending too much on a too-fancy gown.

Make sure the gown is of good quality. Inspect the seams and stitches to ensure that it's been made well. You don't want your investment to fall apart on you.

Buy a simpler gown. Beads and bangles raise the price of the gown and the care it requires. If you like the beaded look, you can always add your own or have a friend do the work for you. Tammy bought a simple gown for two hundred dollars and bought fifty dollars worth of pearls and beads to stitch onto her neckline and bodice. When she was finished, her wedding gown looked identical to an eight-hundred-dollar store-bought wedding gown.

Buy a gown in a less expensive material. Do your homework on fabric prices. Compare satin, taffeta, silk, crisp cotton, etc.

A shorter, tea-length, or suit dress is of course going to be less expensive than a full-length gown with a ten-foot train. Just make sure it fits the formality of your wedding.

Shop the sales, particularly after-holiday sales. Also included in this discount category is the sale rack on which you'll find discontinued gowns, sample gowns marked down, and last season's still-fabulous styles the store is trying to move out.

Did you ever think while you were walking through a regular dress shop, "I wish this pretty white dress was a wedding dress. It would be perfect for me."? Well, get it and turn it into a wedding dress. Just because the pretty white dress is on the prom gown rack, the bridesmaid's rack, or even the New Year's special rack doesn't mean it won't do. No one said the label has to read "Certified Wedding Gown" in order for you to wear it to your wedding. In fact, since everything labeled with the words *wedding* or *bridal* is by nature elevated in price, you're saving money just by looking in the non–bridal dress section. And wouldn't it be wonderful to buy your wedding gown for under a hundred dollars?

If you find that a full-priced gown on a dress shop rack has a tiny, fixable flaw, ask the store manager if you can have that gown for a discount. After all, other brides might not take it in its current condition. A flawed gown can always be mended. So don't walk past that "irregular" rack, either.

Maya, a bride-to-be, found a pretty off-white gown that had a torn side seam. A simple repair would do the trick, *she* knew, but the store considered it damaged goods and knocked seventy-five dollars off the price just to get it off their rack.

Ask the manager when the new shipment of gowns is scheduled to arrive. With advance notice, you might be able to beat the crowds for the nicest but most inexpensive in the bunch.

Don't trust a sale sign without checking to see if the price is really better. The thousand-dollar price tag you see marked out in red pen, then replaced with a seven-hundred-fifty-dollar tag may just be a ploy to make you think you're getting a huge discount. This is where comparison shopping is crucial.

Shop early in the day. You have more energy for comparison shopping, and you're more likely to be focused on the one job at hand.

Look in your Yellow Pages for outlet stores, and head out for a day of sure-thing cut prices up to 60 percent, 70 percent, even 80 percent off. If you're near a Jessica McClintock Gunne Sax outlet, you're set. Brides-to-be have found beautiful gowns for as little as twenty or thirty dollars at the outlets. To find outlets near you, or to learn more about the benefits of outlet shopping, write, call, or check your library or bookstore for these publications:

The Joy of Outlet Shopping
The Outlet Consumer Reporter
P.O. Box 7867
St. Petersburg, FL 33734

Outlet Bound 800-336-8853

Believe it or not, some of the most beautiful ivory and off-white gowns can be found at antique shops. Krissy, a bride, found a 1930 antique hand-beaded wedding dress for under two hundred dollars. Scout the ones in the center of town, ask for help (most antique-store owners are aware of what's in stock in other antique stores), and even browse through some of the antique shows you've seen advertised in the paper.

While you may not be thrilled at the idea of buying your wedding gown at a garage sale—it may be laughable to you, in fact—you'll find great prices for gowns that have been worn only once or twice and need just a cleaning and some alteration. The bridal gowns of women who, for some reason, never made it down the aisle are sold at some garage sales brand-new for a fraction of their original price. So keep an eye out for garage sales that advertise wedding gowns as highlight merchandise. One bride found her wedding gown while driving home from work. The garage sale she almost passed featured a simple wedding gown in a cleaner's bag hanging from a tree branch. She immediately snapped up the gown—an unused designer style—for twenty-five dollars.

Again, it may seem unthinkable for you to order your bridal gown from a catalog, but it's not so strange when you realize that's exactly what you're doing indirectly when you order a gown at a store. Only this way, your refund policy is better. So don't skip the bridal pages of catalogs like JCPenney's that show up in the mail. Compare prices and looks with your other possibilities, and give the book a fair chance to help you out.

When choosing your gown, no matter where you're shopping, always consider your body type and whether that dress is right for you. Does it make you look shorter? Is it accentuating your hips? Is it too tight? Is it too low cut?

Order your correct dress size according to the manufacturer's measurements so you won't have to pay for major alterations. Some dress shops order larger sizes intentionally so the buyer has to pay to have the dress taken in. Similarly, don't order a dress size smaller than what you are right now because you're planning to lose thirty pounds by your wedding day. At worst, you won't lose all the weight and you'll be stuck with a too small gown that doesn't look good on you. Instead, order your current size and don't worry about the cost of alterations.

Having my dress taken in when I lost only half the weight I wanted to actually cheered me up a lot. I couldn't wait to tell my fiancé that the dress had to be taken in.

—*Pam, bride.*

Order a wedding gown that can be cut to a shorter length, trimmed of embellishments, and worn again. It's good money sense to spend that much for a dress you *will* be able to wear again.

Don't leave deposits on several gowns in different stores when you're just looking. You may not get that money back, and there's really no need to believe the saleswoman who's trying to get you to believe a busload of brides might just order up every last one in the next day or two. Leave a deposit only when you're sure.

When paying for your gown, use a credit card. You'll have an easier time getting reimbursed if something should go wrong.

Keep all sales slips as a record of the date you ordered the dress, the specifics of the dress and its size and, as added precaution, get the salesperson to sign it as a record of who sold the dress to you. Trouble can be cleared up easily with that information.

Keep a record of the promised date of delivery, too, so you can get on the phone if your dress is late.

If you're not the type to feel strongly about keeping your wedding gown forever and having it preserved for future generations, you can save a bundle by renting your wedding gown. The practice is catching on with those who can't justify spending several hundred dollars on a dress they'll wear once, and the horror of it is diminishing by those more traditional. Check the Yellow Pages and get ready to save. Just make sure they allow you to pick up the gown way in advance for your fitting and peace of mind.

For the ultimate savings and sentimentality, wear your mother's wedding gown. Or your grandmother's. Or your stepmother's. Cleaning and alteration costs are minimal, and there's no way to put a price tag on the way you'll all feel when you appear in a gown that has so much meaning to your family. As an added coup, you might even consider asking *his* mother if she'd allow you to wear her gown. (That is, of course, if she has no daughters who might resent your taking the honor away from them.) Or even ask your sister or a close relative or friend if she'd allow you to wear her wedding gown on your wedding day.

If you've got the know-how and the equipment, buy some fabric and a pattern and make the gown yourself. Or enlist the services of a talented friend or relative and have her make the gown for you as a gift. You provide the materials, and if necessary, the machine, and she does the tough part. Or have a student at a nearby fashion institute or college fashion department make the gown for you. Maybe it could be a senior project for college credit or a portfolio project. It's still a savings of hundreds of dollars to you. Linda, a recent bride, saved one hundred seventy-five dollars by commissioning her sister's fashion institute friends to make her gown from a sketch she'd drawn. A professional designer would have charged her three hundred to five hundred dollars, she later learned.

Seamstresses can be hired to make the gown for you from scratch. You provide the material and pattern, of course, and then pay her for the work. This custom method of creating your dress may not bring as much savings as some of the other ideas, but it's a definite chop off the store-bought prices you'll find.

Some seamstresses do a little bit of moonlighting. Several travel to big cities on buyer's trips, frequenting discount shops, showrooms, designers, and secondhand boutiques in trendier areas in search of simple and inexpensive wedding dresses to mend and embellish to sell for profit. Call around to see if any nearby seamstresses perform that service, and then arrange to take a look. You may even find the occasional designer original with a price you can manage. The seamstress who worked on the author's wedding gown took her up to her projects room and showed her her collection of thirty wedding gowns she found for less than wholesale at the showroom sale: all were to be fixed up and sold for half their full retail price. The author called all her friends and alerted them to this gold mine.

During fittings, ensure the correct fit by wearing the bra, slip, and shoes you'll be wearing on your wedding day. They can affect the way the dress hangs on you and save you money on last-minute alterations. And *always* get receipts for your fittings.

One bride unfortunately had to pay fifty dollars in last-minute alteration fees at her final fitting because her selection of wedding underwear made the dress a little too snug. Yet another bride found that her new thirty-dollar corset-style strapless bra was just enough to keep the back zipper on her gown from closing all the way so she had to do without.

14

Your Shoes and Accessories

Sometimes all the pieces of your outfit can add up to cost more than the dress itself. Here's how to keep accessory and shoe cost low:

Your Shoes

Don't order shoes in a bridal salon. The price will be much higher than in a regular shoe store. One price test turned up a fifty-dollar difference in identical shoes sold at a regular store versus a bridal salon. Some good retail stores to price-quote are: Shoetown, Kinney, and Thom McAn.

For a great price cut, order the same style shoes your bridesmaids will be wearing so you're a part of their group order discount. Yours may even be free with a group order of, say, four pairs or more. Just be sure your pair isn't sent on to be dyed with theirs.

The top priority in the choice of your shoes, since they'll most likely be hidden for most of the day, is comfort. Choose a style and heel height that won't make you feel all blistered and sore.

Choose plain shoes over fancy, decorated ones. Each bead and sewn-in design costs money. If you must have fancy shoes, plain styles can be adorned with your mother's old clip-on shoe decorations or through your own skill with a glue gun and decorating materials.

Beaded, appliquéd shoes	$75
Plain ½″ heel shoes	$29

Look in the Yellow Pages for a discount shoe store and shop there. Inspect your choices for quality as well as price. A fifteen-dollar pair of shoes is no bargain if they fall part after two uses.

Look for seasonal shoe sales. A 50 percent clearance will take the bite out of shoe prices.

Wear ballerina slippers. They're light and comfortable, they look charming and romantic, and they're inexpensive as well. At the right store or in a dancer's supply catalog, like Capezio, you can find these for as low as ten dollars a pair. Look in your Yellow Pages under Dancing Supplies.

Check out a few antique stores for those pretty antique lace-up boots. You might just beat the prices offered in bridal salons and lingerie catalogs.

Consider the plain shoes sold at discount in family-style catalogs such as Montgomery Wards (800-852-2711) and JCPenney (800-222-6161). Just make sure the company has a good return policy in case the style or fit is not right for you.

Shop for your shoes later in the afternoon when your feet are naturally swollen. Shoes that fit in the morning may be tight on you during your evening reception, so think ahead and use a general rule of shoe shopping.

While trying on shoes, be sure you're wearing stockings rather than socks. Either wear your own, or if you're caught without and have just found a great sale, use the footsie stockings available to shoe store patrons for this very purpose. It's a good idea to carry your own pair of knee-highs or footsie stockings in your purse when you're shoe shopping.

For the ultimate in savings, wear a pair of white dress shoes you already own. Just make sure they look nice, not old, scraped, and worn in the heel. You will be lifting up your dress to reveal your garter later on in the reception, and you won't want to reveal your savings in the shoe department at the same time. Fix up a nice pair of your shoes, perhaps with some polish, and you're all set.

Scuff up the bottoms of your shoes for traction, and wear your shoes around the house for a few days before the wedding to break them in. You don't want stiff, slippery shoes on your wedding day. Better to be safe and comfortable than not.

Your Veil

The veil you'll wear depends on the formality of your wedding and the dress you'll be wearing, so avoid having to return your choice for a loss of money by being sure of the basics before you shop. Comparison shop for veils in bridal salons' sale racks. You won't have to sacrifice frugality for selection. Or look through bridal and discount catalogs for a reasonably priced veil.

Check the classified ads for used wedding veils. A once-worn piece originally bought for several hundred dollars in a bridal salon (sometimes more than the price of a wedding gown) can be found for sale by the owner for just a fraction of that price.

Veils can be rented, if you're not superstitious about previously worn wedding attire. Check the Yellow Pages.

Wear your mother's wedding veil. It will mean a lot to both of you, and you'll probably only have to pay for a cleaning and alteration to your height. Or borrow a relative's veil if she seems receptive to the idea. Siblings, grandmothers, godmothers, great-grandparents—all are likely to bestow the honor.

Have a talented relative or friend make your veil for you, using a fabric headband, some pearls, netting. Tear out a picture of the kind of veil you'd like, and accept the artist's work as her gift to you. Or make your own veil if you have the time and the talent. One bride's aunt recently made the bride's veil from some tulle, a fabric headband, and some pearls. Her gorgeous creation cost just thirty dollars to make and was even prettier than the two-hundred-dollar styles in stores.

For informal or nonreligious weddings, it may be appropriate for you to go without a veil. Check your etiquette books, search your options, and decide.

Your Headcovering

Rather than a veil and headpiece, choose instead a lovely and inexpensive single flower tucked behind your ear. Clip the flower from your bouquet or cut it from your garden.

An arrangement of baby rosebuds and baby's breath can be tucked into a hairclip that holds up a French twist. There's no need to order this to be made at extra cost by your florist; just experiment ahead of time and do it yourself.

A plain hat might be found on sale, and it can be worn as is or embellished with ribbons and flowers. Either way, you're still going to beat the price of a bridal hat sold in a salon, which can cost two to three times more.

Or choose instead not to wear any headcovering at all. Just make sure this option conforms to your wedding location's rules and the degree of formality of the wedding.

Your Slip

Don't buy your slip in a bridal salon if you can help it. By now you must have realized that bridal salons are far more expensive than your other options. Check in department store bridal and undergarment departments for slips and skirts that will do just as nicely . . . for one-half to one-third of what you would have spent in the bridal salon.

Borrow your mother's bridal slip and skirts. Perhaps she still has hers around, and it can be your "something borrowed."

Make your own slip, or alter one given to you by a relative or friend.

Do you really need a slip? Check your dress out in all lighting—indoors, outdoors, direct sunlight, spotlights—to see if you can get away with wearing one less layer.

Your Garter

Since you'll undoubtedly want to keep your garter as a precious memento of your wedding day, you should have two garters: one to keep and one to throw. Buy what brides call a "cheapie" in a lingerie store for the tossing, and use your mother's wedding garter as yours to keep (if she'll pass it down to you).

Or make your own garter with a length of elastic, satin, lace, and some ribbons. The cost: barely ten dollars, depending on where you shop for materials. Compare that to bridal salon pricetags of twenty-five dollars or more.

Your Stockings and Lingerie

Buy basic stockings. While the fancy silk kinds with patterns or the little design at the ankle are great indulgences for the bride, they're also a place where money can be saved without noticeable loss. You'll feel just as wonderful on your wedding day whether your stockings cost forty dollars or not. One option is to order your stockings from a catalog of discounted irregulars. (Try L'Eggs Brands, Inc., P.O. Box 748, Rural Hall, NC 27098.)

Sexy, silky lingerie under your gown can make you even more radiant on your wedding day, but you can save money on your bra, teddy, panties, or G-string. Rather than buy a new set for you wedding day, wear the lacy white number you already have, or use the Victoria's Secret gift certificate you received at your shower.

Shop for your wedding bra and panties in catalogs or in discount stores, or watch for clearance sales at Victoria's Secret. They offer two-for-one sales, half-off prices, and free gifts with purchases. Call 800-888-8200 to order a catalog.

Don't wear a bra under your gown. How's that for savings?

> *Not only is it one less check to write, the lack of a bra may also help get the zipper up over your back easier. It did for me, and I was so much more comfortable without it. Thank goodness my dress was so thick and detailed that no one knew I didn't have one on.*
>
> *—Lisa, bride.*

Have an extra pair of stockings in your emergency bag (more on this later) in case of a noticeable run. If you have splurged on expensive silk stockings for your originals, this definitely should be the more generic of the two you've purchased.

Skip all the extras, like gloves and parasols. They're the essence of nonessential. One bride's total for gloves, a parasol, and jeweled hairclips for under her veil: one hundred eighty dollars. That amount could be better used elsewhere. Like the honeymoon.

Your Jewelry

Don't buy new jewelry for your wedding. It's very likely that your groom's wedding gift to you will be fine jewelry of some sort, and you'll want to wear that.

> *I didn't know Michael had already bought me a pearl necklace to wear on our wedding day, and unfortunately I went out and bought myself one on sale too. It couldn't be returned.*
>
> *—Carrie, bride.*

Jewelry, if not a gift, also makes a wonderful "something borrowed" choice. Wear an heirloom necklace or earrings, perhaps the pearls your mother wore at her own wedding.

Cash Bag

Rather than buy an expensive beaded bag in which to keep the cards and checks given to you by guests at your wedding, make a simple satin bag yourself or . . . borrow a relative's or friend's decorative cash bag. Older, discolored ones can be cleaned carefully.

> *With a little work, the beaded bag my grandmother made for my mother's wedding gradually lost its yellow color and I was able to use it with my white gown. If I were to buy a beaded bag like that one today, I would have easily spent three hundred dollars, more if I had searched for an antique.*
> *—Barb, bride.*

15

Dressing the Bridal Party

Bridesmaids and Junior Bridesmaids

The Bridesmaids' Gowns

While some brides like to purchase their bridesmaids' gowns as a gift for them, you'd do well to allow them to buy their own dresses. Most expect that they'll have to anyway.

Look at the bridesmaids gowns shown in magazines to get a feel for the current styles and colors, and call the printed toll-free numbers of the stores listed in the advertisements for the price range.

Resources for Bridesmaids' Gowns

Alfred Angelo	1075 Broken Sound Parkway
	Boca Raton FL 33487
Bridal Originals	800-876-GOWN
Eden	818-441-8715
Galina Bouquet	212-564-1020
Jessica McClintock	800-333-5301
Joelle	212-736-8811
Laura Ashley	800-223-6917
Bill Levkoff	800-LEVKOFF
Lanz	800-421-0731
New Image	800-421-IMAGE

Your research will be a great help when it's time to go dress hunting.

Just as you were encouraged to order your gown directly from the manufacturer listed in the advertisement in a bridal magazine, you can do the same for your maids' gowns to be sure you're not getting a copy at original prices.

Go with your maids to the dress shop so that you'll all have a say in the dresses they'll be wearing. You'll want them to choose a dress to match the formality of your wedding and to complement your gown, and they'll want to make sure a completely unflattering style and color is not chosen for them. One bride, for instance, chose a dress for all four of her attendants. The two women with larger-than-average chests looked even larger, and the other two looked like sticks. No one was happy, especially at one hundred thirty dollars a dress.

Always hunt for group discounts when you're looking for bridesmaids' dresses. Ask even if one isn't offered. Marisa, a recent bride, made the question of group discounts a part of her search and comparisons of stores. When she found a company that offered group discounts, each of her attendants saved 20 percent on their dresses.

Look in department stores for your maids' gowns. Prices there, as mentioned before, are likely to be much lower than those in the bridal shops. Also look in smaller dress shops for better prices and perhaps better service.

Prom and party dresses are very often ordered as bridesmaids' gowns. Just be sure to shop outside of prom season, because prices may be elevated due to demand. The best time to shop may be pre-pre-prom season and post-prom season when dressy dresses are overstocked and up for clearance. The brides panel found pretty bridesmaids' dresses on the post-prom rack for as low as thirty dollars, marked down from one hundred twenty dollars.

Shop at outlets, perhaps when you're hunting through the Gunne Sax outlet for your own gown. Again, researchers found dresses at 50 percent to 60 percent off.

If you have only one or two bridesmaids, you might find complementary gowns in an antique shop for a fraction of what salons charge for the "heirloom look."

Wherever you're shopping, encourage the maids to choose a gown style according to their budget, not yours. You'll all feel better.

Encourage your maids to choose a style of dress they'll be able to wear again to formal dinners, dances, and the like. A hundred-dollar dress is a better deal when it's used ten times.

Keep in mind that simpler dresses are often less expensive than detailed, sexy ones. Aside from the price, the maids shouldn't look provocative on your wedding day.

Consider having your maids rent their dresses. Ultraformal gowns can be found for the price of casuals. No one has to know the dresses are rented.

Shop at bridal shops that offer free alterations. If the bridal shop charges for its alteration package, you might choose to pass. Either have a bridesmaid with sewing experience do the job herself, or ask a relative or friend to help.

If the tailoring job is just too involved, perhaps you can find a good seamstress to hire for much less than the dress shop's rates. Get references and comparison shop. Savings here can be anywhere from fifty to a hundred dollars.

A friend or relative with sewing experience, or an inexpensive seamstress, could create gowns for your maids at little more than the cost of material and a pattern. Consider the old-fashioned way for outstanding savings, but be sure your worker has just as much talent as willingness to help. A twenty-dollar gown can look like a hundred-dollar gown when it's done right, but it can also look like a five-dollar gown if it's not.

If you have a talented dressmaker lined up, you can save even more money on materials. Look for markdowns on fabric and lace, beads, and other items. Just be sure to inspect all materials thoroughly so you don't discover later a hidden reason for that fabulous sale price.

Ask your bridesmaids, mother, relatives, and friends to keep an eye out for fabric sales where they live. One bride received a call from a cousin in San Diego who found a clearance sale on fabric and lace. The bride placed an order with her cousin, paid her for the purchase and shipping, and still saved seventy-five dollars.

If your bridesmaids all live in different cities, have them send you their professionally taken measurements on size cards and checks for their dresses. Then you take those size cards to the dress shop you've chosen so that you can order your maids' gowns for them.

Do not allow your maids to order their gowns in shops near their homes, because batches of gowns may differ in hue according to which factory they were made in. Always order the gowns in one place, then send them out to your maids.

Send the gowns first class and insure them when you mail them to your maids. This is no time for a dress to get lost in the mail. If you're nervous about this, ask your bridesmaids to let you know when their packages arrive. Or attach return postcards on each package so you'll be notified of safe delivery.

As an alternative to this setup, assign your maid of honor the task of ordering and delivering gowns, especially if she lives close to the bridesmaids while you're far from home. One bride saved over fifty dollars in shipping and communications this way.

Shoes

Comparison shop at different shoe stores and research the prices of those styles you see in the magazines.

For the same reason that gowns must be, shoes must also be ordered in the same place. Differences in shoe colors among your maids can ruin your bridal party's look, so arrange to order as a group. The best way to do this is to pick out a shoe style at a national chain of shoe stores, get the style number from the clerk, then ask your maids to go and try on that particular shoe in the same chain's stores near them. You know that a size seven in one style may be the same as a nine in another, so it's best to help your maids order shoes that will fit them correctly. Once the maids have their sizes in the style you've chosen, you can more accurately order their shoes for them.

Try for a group discount when you're ordering shoes. Talk to the manager if you have to. It's possible that your pair of shoes could be given to you free if your order is large enough.

Rather than mailing the shoes to your maids, consider holding onto them at your house so they won't have to travel with bulky shoe boxes to your place for the wedding. Give the shoes to your maids a few days before the wedding so they can break them in and scuff the soles a bit to prevent slipping.

A pretty alternative to the dyed high-heeled shoe: ballerina slippers. If they look right with the dresses and are consistent with the formality of the wedding, they'll be a huge savings and much less trouble.

Headpieces

In place of costly headpieces, use the material cut from the bottoms of the bridesmaids' gowns as ribbons for the maids' hair.

Decorate the maids' French-braided or upswept hairstyles with wisps of baby's breath.

If you like the idea of your maids wearing flowers in their hair, consider using some of the baby's breath from their own bouquets or cut some sprigs from your own garden. Most florists charge for blooms intended for your bridesmaids' hair, but you can beat that cost with a pair of scissors and some creative clipping.

Have each maid bring her own string of pearls—fake or genuine—to her beauty appointment so the stylist can incorporate the strand into her French braid.

It's perfectly fine for your maids not to adorn their hair at all. In fact, it's quite classy.

Slips and Stockings

Allow each maid to wear her own slip (of an appropriate length and color) under her gown. There's no need for your attendants to buy new undergarments for your wedding.

For a uniform look, though, your maids should wear the same brand and color stockings. Either take their order and pick up two pairs for each maid, or have your maid of honor do this for you. A good way to save money on stockings (up to 50 percent) is to choose plain pairs over the fancy, silky, name-brand styles. For discount stocking, see the resource in Chapter 14. (Keep the stockings at your house so everyone has the right stockings waiting for them when they arrive on the morning of the wedding.)

Accessories

Inexpensive gloves may be found at department stores if you look for them. Those you see at bridal salons are probably overpriced, so check elsewhere first.

If your wedding isn't a formal one, you may choose not to have your maids wear gloves.

Also, skip the pricey extras such as parasols and fans.

Flower Girls

Flower-Girl Dresses

Their mothers usually buy the flower girls' dresses, so do Mom a favor by suggesting an inexpensive style the little girls can use again.

Your flower girls can get a second wearing out of their First Communion or party dresses. Either leave the dresses unadorned or incorporate your color scheme through the use of gloves, ribbons, lace, a sash, or trim. For the price of just a fabric sash (eight dollars) flower girl Lauren's fancy white party dress became her dress for the wedding. She saved her family fifty-five dollars by not needing a new dress for that day.

Have your flower girls' dresses made, either by a talented relative, a friend, or an inexpensive seamstress. And shop at fabric sales for the material for the flower girls' dresses. You won't need much. A smart shopper can assemble supplies for each flower-girl dress for twenty dollars per dress.

Shoes

Flower girls may wear their own party shoes or their dancing school ballet slippers.

Headpieces

Wreaths of flowers look charming on the heads of flower girls, so consider this simple look for your own. Skip the florists' charge for a child's headdress and make the wreaths yourself using some florist wire, blooms, and ribbon.

Florist's price	$40
Homemade	$15

Accessories

Borrow a basket from a friend for each flower girl to carry during the ceremony.

The Groom, the Groomsmen, and the Fathers of the Bride and Groom

As the men will most likely be wearing identical tuxedos or similar suits, they're all grouped together here. This condensed listing is of course not to reflect any diminished importance of the men involved in the wedding process.

The Tuxedo or Suit

Again, look at plenty of pictures in magazines and brochures to get an idea of the colors, fabrics, styles, and prices that suit your group best. Look at a picture of the tuxedo next to a picture of the bridesmaids' gowns. Make sure they look good together.

Ask recently married friends if they'd recommend the tuxedo rental shop they used for their wedding. This way, you'll have an idea of the business's reliability and quality.

Always compare prices at tuxedo rental agencies around town. Companies to look for in your phone book are those that offer Gingiss Formalwear, Lord West, Henry Grethel, etc.

Look for a reputable tuxedo rental agency that offers group discounts.

Ask if the groom gets his tuxedo free with your grooms-men's order or if, when the groom will be wearing a military uniform, the free tux can go to your father.

If the groomsmen and the fathers of the bride and groom are many miles away at the time of the tuxedo order, have the men send in their measurements on size cards so the correct tuxedos can be ordered for them. Be sure they get their measurements taken at a professional tailor's shop—again, no ruler and string job—so that the numbers are reliable.

Schedule tailoring for several days before the wedding . . . in case of a problem. If a problem were to be found at the last minute, extra charges would be made for rushed alterations.

If the men will be wearing dark suits, their minor expense will be identical ties. Look in a discount store or at a department store sale for these. Check Marshall's, Today's Man, or NBO for good values.

Make sure you get a signed copy of the contract or order receipt to verify your order in case of a mix-up. Record the style number, style name, sizes, deposit amount, check number, delivery date, and the name of the clerk who took your tuxedo order. Good record keeping ensures that any questions or mistakes made by the tuxedo agency can be cleared up quickly. Call several times to confirm the order and availability of the tuxedos—just to make sure.

If your groomsmen will be wearing dark suits instead of tuxedos, as in the case of an informal wedding, the men will undoubtedly be wearing suits they already own. But just to be sure their look will be appropriate, arrange for the men to wear the suits ahead of time for you (perhaps to a dinner party). This way, you can check to see that their version of dark is really dark, that the suits are in good order and style, and that leg and arm lengths aren't too short. You have a right to preview what the men will be wearing, so if they complain about the scrutiny, just tell them that the plans could be changed if they wish. They could always shell out for a tuxedo. You won't believe how quickly they'll have their suits tailored.

Shoes

Shoes can be rented at a group discount rate at the tuxedo rental shop.

The men can wear their own dark shoes if the dark suits will be their wedding-day wardrobe. Again, arrange to see the shoes ahead of time.

Ring Bearers

Suits

If the boy will be renting a tuxedo, try to get a discount at the store you've chosen as your men's outfitter.

Allow the ring bearer to wear his own little suit, with a new bow tie to match the bridal party's color scheme.

A little boy's version of a tuxedo can be sewn from a pattern. Enlist the help of a talented friend, relative, or inexpensive seamstress to make the boy's wedding-day clothing.

As many brides know, the young ring bearer will look adorable in white shorts and a white shirt with a little cummerbund and a bow tie. The clothes may be his own, while the tie and cummerbund may be made with ease. This is a popular new practice, as it is both a charming look and a big savings.

Shoes

Find a child's discount shoe store and look for an inexpensive style, or the ring bearer may wear a pair of his own dress shoes if they're appropriate.

16

Dressing the Mothers of the Bride and Groom

The Dress

Look through magazines with your mother so both of you can discuss what kinds of dresses will be appropriate, which colors you prefer. This way, you won't have to accompany your mother to every dress shop she wants to "just take a look in," and you won't have to fear her choice when she announces she's found the perfect dress.

Remember the mothers' dresses should adhere to the formality of your wedding. That means long gowns are out if the bridesmaids are wearing tea-length dresses. In essence, the mothers of the bride and groom are an extended part of the bridal party, so wardrobe rules apply to them as well. Besides, shorter, less formal gowns usually aren't as expensive as those floor-length, beaded numbers.

The mothers' gowns should be somewhat conservative in order not to outdo the bride's, so you're also avoiding the extra expense of a flashier style.

Avoid bridal salons for the mothers' dresses. As you know by now, prices here are often much higher than those of nonspecialized dress shops. Look in the formal section of a regular department store. Prices are bound to be lower than in the salon, and you may chance upon a sale. Identical gowns were seen in a bridal salon priced at two hundred fifty dollars and at a regular dress shop for one hundred seventy-five dollars.

Speaking of sales, shop for the mothers' gowns after major holidays. After-event overstock may be reduced in price for clearance.

Consider shopping for the mother of the bride's and the mother of the groom's dresses in an outlet store for a considerable discount. You'll find savings up to 60 percent off or more in some national outlets.

Flip through formalwear catalogs.

Encourage both your mother and his mother to make their own gowns, if they are both inclined to do so. They may just need permission from you to do what they really wanted to do in the first place. And skip expensive alteration charges by doing the tailoring yourself, or by having the others tailor their own dresses. A helpful friend or relative could also help out.

Buy a very simple gown in a department or discount store and add a jeweled neckline or fancy trim.

Check into formal dress rentals for both mothers, a much less expensive alternative to buying.

If the groom's mother lives far away from you or your mother, send her a swatch and a picture of the gown your mother has chosen so she can then make her selection. The mother of the bride chooses her dress first as an honor, and the mother of the groom should wear a similar but not identical style and a similar color. It looks better in the wedding photos if the mothers are in complementary rather than clashing colors.

The Shoes

Avoid shoe selection at the bridal salon. They may be overpriced. Instead, comparison shop among the larger shoe chains in your area.

Order the mothers' shoes with yours and your bridesmaids' for an even better group discount rate, if available. Remember to ask.

Encourage them to buy simpler shoes and adorn them with clip-on decorations or glue-on beads.

Accessories

To save them money, encourage your mother and his mother to wear their own jewelry and to forgo headpieces or hats.

Except perhaps in ultraformal weddings, gloves are optional for the mothers of the bride and groom. They may even be inappropriate for a less formal wedding. So decide what would look best, and if gloves are indeed included, either look for good discounts, or allow the mothers of the bride and groom to wear gloves they already own.

17

Keepsakes

To record your planning experiences—which are always fun to look back on—keep a journal in a plain, lined notebook. The fancy bridal journals on the market are not one page longer than these and they do the same job, yet they may be double or triple in cost.

Bridal journals	$20–$30
Plain journal	$5–$10

❧

Charge up the home video camera and take your own footage throughout the wedding-planning months and on the morning of the wedding. It's ridiculous to pay a professional photographer to record your rehearsal and the four hours it takes to get everyone ready before the ceremony. Besides, home movies are far more personal and fun than those taken by a stranger.

Make your own wedding memorabilia scrapbox, in which you'll put swatches of material, favors, menus, and all the little meaningful items you wouldn't dare throw away. Bridal stores sell these types of decorated memorabilia boxes, but you can beat their price by covering a large cardboard box with either satiny material or bridal wrapping paper, lace, ribbons, bows, and a print label of the contents.

Store-bought memorabilia box	$40–60
Homemade box	$5–$20

If you don't have room or enough keepsakes for a memorabilia box, make your own wedding scrapbook instead. Again, you'll do better to make your own rather than to buy one in a bridal store (just cover a plain photo album with material, lace, and perhaps a pretty little picture frame attached to the front cover). You can keep all the notes, swatches, samples of perfume, and pictures you'll treasure years from now in this book.

Store-bought bridal scrapbook	$20–$30
Homemade bridal scrapbook	$10–$15

Save copies of the letters you've written to update your bridal party and the letters you and your fiancé have written to one another during the planning of your wedding. No need for those specially ordered computer-printed love notes you can buy through catalogs. The real thing will do fine.

If your photo-developing store offers double prints for the same price as singles, or a free enlargement, take the opportunity to save money on prints you'd otherwise have to make for relatives and friends anyway.

Printed napkins and matchboxes are keepsakes that can be cut out. If you find these nonessentials necessary, however, take extra care to comparison shop in discount stationery stores and at print shops to get the best bargain possible. Include in your price research those items that may be offered by the reception hall as well. In some instances, they may even be offered as freebies. Check well.

18

How Many Guests?

Make it clear that the guest limits for each side are firm numbers so that neither side overextends, thinking they can just slide by. Make it known how serious you are and you'll avoid the tensions of overstepped boundaries. Too many brides have been pushed into accepting "just three more" over and over—and at thirty to fifty dollars per person, the figures add up.

If you have to invite many guests, plan a more informal reception so that the cost of meals per person is reduced.

Once the lists are drawn, go down each column marking "definites" and "maybes." You'll know better where to begin your cuts should your original guest-list numbers be too high for your budget. Obviously, the fewer guests you invite, the less you'll have to pay for your reception. However, don't make your guest list too small. You'll insult relatives and friends by excluding them, and you'll also feel that you've ripped yourself off when there's next to nobody passing through the receiving line. Just work toward the point of a fair and comfortable medium.

Don't invite children. With the wording of your invitation, you're aware, you indicate to your guests that their children are not invited to the wedding. When you're paying fifty dollars per person, it makes sense to leave out the fifteen toddlers and infants who won't even eat their very expensive meals. Yes, many formal halls count each body present as a full-price person. Ask the manager of your location if this is the case.

Don't allow teenagers and uncommitted daters to bring their own guests to your wedding. This will be evident in the wording of the invitation, but if a person indicates to you that she's planning to bring a date, it's your right to remind her that space limitations prevent you from letting her bring a guest. Tell her how your sister, the maid of honor, isn't even bringing a guest. If a response card is returned to you with a written-in addition of a guest's escort—an entirely inappropriate move not cleared with you first—call the offender and tactfully remind him or her that space on the guest list does not allow additional people to be invited to the wedding. Don't be manipulated into paying for this extra person when your college roommates, your boss, and your second cousins all had to be left off the list.

If you have many relatives, friends, and clients you just won't be able to invite to the wedding, plan an additional party for all either a week before the wedding or after your return from your honeymoon. Make it clear than no gifts are necessary, so that no charges of greed are leveled against you. The important thing is to celebrate with your closest acquaintances.

This is a sticky one with etiquette mavens, but you really don't have to invite the wedding officiant to the reception if you're not close to him or her. An officiant hired to perform the ceremony has already been paid a fee, so you shouldn't feel pressured to shell out another hundred bucks to invite him or her to your party, too.

When looking at price per head, keep in mind that you may have to feed the entertainment. A DJ is only one person and only one price, while a full band may cost you twelve full meals. It's best to keep the numbers low.

When expenses look like they could start getting out of hand, it's time to start cutting the guest list. Begin with those marked as "maybes."

Cut those guests who have drifted from you in the past few months and years.

Cut old high school and college friends you're sure you'll never see again.

Cut people you're inviting simply because you were invited to their wedding fifteen years ago . . . but you haven't seen or spoken to them more than three times since.

Cut your parents' friends and clients who don't really know you.

Cut a whole level of guests—such as all second cousins.

Ask the groom's family to cut their guests equally. This is tough to do, so compromise as much as possible.

Don't send invitations to faraway relatives with the idea that they won't be able to make it and you're just sending the invitation to be nice. They might decide to hop a plane and attend after all, and then you have to add on a handful of guests you hadn't counted on. One bride was shocked when overseas relatives responded that all ten of them would attend her wedding. Her advice: "Be careful who you invite; they just may show up."

19

Invitations

The formality of your wedding is reflected in your invitations. So choose invitations that match the style of your wedding. Even formal invitations can still be found for bargain prices.

Know exactly how many invitations you will need so you can comparison shop with the applicable numbers.

As you know already, shop around in several different stationery stores to get the best prices available. Comparison shop like crazy. Send for free catalogs and borrow those of recently married friends.

Resources for Invitation Research

American Wedding Album	800-428-0379
Crane	800-IS CRANE
Dawn	800-528-6677
Evangel	800-342-4227
Jamie Lee	800-288-5800
Jenner	502-222-0191
Invitation Hotline	800-800-4355
Now & Forever	800-451-8616
Precious Collection	800-553-9080
Rexcraft	800-635-4653
Sugar 'n Spice	800-635-1433
Wedding Treasures	800-851-5974
Willow Tree Lane	800-219-9230

Note: For additional savings of up to 30 percent, contact Informals at 800-6-INVITE with the catalog book and model number of the invitation you like. This company offers discounts on retail invitation sales.

When adding up the number of invitations you'll need, follow these rules: Families get their own; those over the age of eighteen get their own; and those inviting a guest get one invitation with both names on it (no need for a separate invitation for the guest).

Plan to order ten to fifteen extras in case of mistakes or replacement guests added to the list when space allows. Leftovers may be kept as mementos.

When figuring your invitation budget, be sure to add in the cost of postage. The two expenses go hand in hand. In most cases, you'll need two first-class stamps per invitation. One hundred invitations, then, equals fifty-eight dollars in postage. International rates are higher.

Take several of those large invitation sample books home with you so you can take a really good look through them and compare prices.

Choose simple, plain, black-and-white invitations rather than the more expensive, fancier ones. Colored inks, borders, pictures, monograms, and laser-cut designs just inflate the price. As an added plus, the simpler the invitations, the classier they look.

Choose thermographed invitations rather than engraved. You won't see much of a difference in style, but they're a much better buy.

Get regular- to small-sized invitations. They're less expensive than oversized ones, and extra postage is not needed for each one.

Get plain envelopes. The colored ones with the printed and shiny liners are all decoration and all added expense.

Choose invitations that are made of thinner paper so you'll pay less in postage.

When looking at catalog prices for invitation packages, be sure to add on the cost of shipping and insurance.

Word your order form carefully and edit several times to check for mistakes. One misspelled word can mean the extra expense of having to reorder if the catalog's low prices mean no returns.

Rather than order professional invitations from a printer or a catalog, you could choose to make your own, using good paper and your high-quality computer and printer. Carefully follow the wording and patterns you see on invitations in wedding books and magazines, and do enclose these in high-quality, matching envelopes with response cards. Or make use of a friend's computer skills and software. This favor can be a wedding gift to you.

If you have connections to an art school, perhaps you'd trust tomorrow's designers to create your invitations for you. Their fee will undoubtedly be little more than the cost of materials and a request for recommendations for their portfolios.

Speaking of the cost of materials, buy your own white or off-white paper at a discount store or in one of those buy-by-the-pound paper warehouses. Get your plain envelopes there, too, remembering that colored papers are generally more expensive than the preferable white and off-white varieties.

Another alternative: Use your computer to draw up the invitation you'd like, and bring a crisp printout to a nearby discount printer to be copied as many times as you need. While it's not as much of a savings as printing the invitations out yourself, it's still less expensive than the professionally printed ones, and you're likely to get outstanding quality.

If you have experience in calligraphy, hand-print a master copy of your invitation. Then either bring this master copy to a discount printer to be duplicated or, if you have the time and patience, you can hand-print in calligraphy all your invitations. It's a classy look if you have the talent, and it's more than a bargain.

If you have little experience in calligraphy but you'd still like to hand-write your own invitation master, buy a simple calligraphy pen and find a guidebook in the library. Spend some time practicing the strokes until you get them right. Perhaps you could work in some extra calligraphy practice by writing up your to-do lists, filling in your journal, and writing letters to your bridal party in the fancy script.

If you'd like the look of calligraphy for your invitations, but don't feel yours would look professional enough in such a short time, ask an artist friend if she'd write out your invitation as her gift to you. Or put up a flier at a local high school or college art department, asking for the services of a calligrapher. Many young artists are just as talented as professionals, and they'd gladly do the job for a fraction of a professional's fee. They also use the work for their portfolios.

Professional calligraphers charge substantial fees for their work, so if you must hire out the job, comparison shop for the best talent at the right price.

Professional calligrapher	$100–$300
Do it yourself	$25 for supplies
A friend's gift to you	Free

Don't order your invitations too early—there may be a last-minute change of date, time, or place. Most brides do well to order their invitations four to six months in advance. By then, everything should be fairly well finalized.

When placing your order, print all information carefully, double-check, have your fiancé double-check, and then check again. Any mistakes you've made in the order will be printed on your invitation, and you'll be stuck with them.

> *When I caught a mistake on my order form, I learned that I had just saved myself two hundred dollars in revision fees.*
> *—Anne, bride.*

Make sure there's a return policy in your contract in case there is a mistake in the printing of the invitations or damage to your order in shipping.

Keep all receipts as proof of purchase, and get the salesperson's name when you place your order. Other information you should record: the date of your order, specifics about the style and amount you're ordering, changes, delivery date, amount or deposit, and further payment obligations. These steps help in case of questions.

Check your invitations carefully when you go to pick them up. If you find mistakes right away, your chances are better for getting them corrected and compensated.

Don't attempt to save a few dollars by not ordering response cards with your invitations. They're the best way to keep a record of how many guests will be in attendance at your wedding. You don't want to have to total up your guest list by *calling* all your relatives and friends.

If your wedding will be less formal, consider including reply postcards with your invitations. Each one costs about ten cents less than a card in an envelope to send through the mail. To make your own bridal postcards, just use regular three-and-half-inch-by-five-inch index cards (the post office recognizes these as postcards) and print out a suitable layout using your computer.

Do not try to save money by not putting return postage on the response card envelopes. That's tacky, and it may send your guests the message that they do not have to return the response cards. Instead, you can save on postage by hand-delivering invitations to friends, co-workers, and close family—anyone with whom you come in contact regularly. One bride saved sixty dollars this way. "Plus, I got to see my friends' excitement when they received their invitations from me."

Mail the invitations early enough so that the response cards will be returned to you several weeks before you have to give the final head count to the caterer. A delay or change could cost you money.

Be sure you have all your guests' names and addresses correct so no invitations are returned to you, leaving an irate aunt who thinks she has been snubbed.

Reception Cards

Rather than order separate reception cards, you may choose just to print the information in the bottom corner of your invitation. Separate cards must be used if you'll invite some guests to the wedding but not the reception.

At-Home Cards

Separate cards that will announce your permanent address, phone number, and even the name you'll be assuming (whether it's his, yours, or a hyphenated combination) are one of those nonessentials that can easily be cut to keep your wedding and postage costs down, especially if your guests already know where you'll be living. This information can be printed on the back of your wedding program.

Thank-You Notes

Rather than order these with your invitations as part of your stationery package, simply use a high-quality plain stationery (not necessarily thank-you or bride's stationery), and hand-write your thank-you in black ink. Comparison shop among discount stationery stores for the best price, taking care to look at price-per-card cost.

Just phoning or printing form-letter thank-yous out on your computer may seem like a savings, but they're actually grievous don'ts in the wedding etiquette world. Just the same, don't use those boxed, fill-in-the-blank thank-you cards. They're not only expensive, they're tacky for wedding thank-yous.

Maps

If you're planning to send maps to your guests who might need help finding the ceremony site and the location of the reception, include the directions with the invitation. There's no sense in sending them separately. Draw your own map or copy a street map for clear directions, then check them well for changes or confusing routes. At one wedding recently, many guests missed the ceremony and arrived just in time for the reception due to the map's omission of a confusing traffic circle.

Copy these maps on a photocopier—yours, a friend's, or the one at work—any one you can use for free. An added tip: Reduce these maps so you can fit four to six to each page. Then copy these six-per sheets at less of a strain on paper or supplies or on your coin supply if you have to pay to use a copier.

Using a pay copier	3¢–5¢ per copy
	$3–$5 for 100
Using a personal copier	free

If your copier will print a larger-sized paper for the same price as a letter-sized paper, use that option to fit more maps to a page.

Of course, send maps only to those guests who need them.

20

Legal Matters

Blood tests are not necessary to get a marriage license in some places, so before you take any tests, find out what is required in your location.

Believe it or not, it may be more expensive to get your blood tests done in some places than in others. So forget about the doctor's office and the twenty-four-hour clinic if they plan to charge you, and look around for a free place like a clinic or a medical school. At the very least, comparison shop for the best price. One bride saved thirty dollars through her research in this area. A document is a document, no matter where the test is taken.

Make sure you have your blood test done at the appropriate time. Depending on your state's rules, these tests are valid only for a certain amount of time. If you miss the window, you'll have to pay to have another done within the allotted time. Also, allow enough time to receive your test results. Many officiants will not sign the needed paperwork for your wedding without these.

Schedule your physicals, if they're required by your state, to coincide with your regular yearly physical. Just be sure to inform your doctor so she can tell you about any rules, regulations, or special tests you'll need. Combining this physical with your annual one can save you up to two hundred dollars in office visit fees in some areas. While you're there, get your immunization shots required for honeymoon travel in some exotic regions, if necessary.

You may be considering writing up a prenuptial agreement. While it may seem a good idea to just write your wishes down and put them in a safe place, your state may require much more legal documentation than that. Consult a legal directory in your library, or place a call to a free legal advice center in your area. If you do need a lawyer for this, comparison shop.

Just like the blood tests, your marriage license is only valid for a certain amount of time. So make sure your ceremony will take place in time, and make sure you can get your marriage license in time. For instance, don't apply for it the day before your wedding. Some states require a twenty-four hour or longer processing time.

If you're planning to take your husband's name or hyphenate your own with his, you have some paperwork to fill out. It may not cost anything to change your name on important documents and accounts, but it could cost you plenty in the long run if your official documents are not amended to stand in order. So be sure to call, write, or otherwise arrange your name change in the following:

Social Security number	Subscriptions
Driver's license	Prescriptions
Credit cards	School records
Bank and loan accounts	Other billing accounts
Bonds	Expense accounts
Telephone cards	Library cards
Telephone account	Other forms of ID

In addition, both you and your partner should have your insurance policies and wills updated to accommodate the change in your lives. In the long run, you'll save time and money by tending to this now.

Let a special relative know that her engagement gift to you was used to pay for your marriage license. That can be a special thrill for the giver, particularly if she originally introduced the two of you or is in any way responsible for your getting married.

> *My eighty-year-old aunt felt badly that she couldn't afford to give us more than twenty-five dollars. But we cheered her up when we told her we used her check for our license. We called it our most important gift.*
>
> *—Ellen, bride.*

21

The Rings

Smart shopping is the rule when you're looking for your wedding bands. Gold and diamonds are high-priced items, so you're not likely to get bargain basement prices anywhere. The best you can do is spend your money wisely, and by all means don't talk yourself into settling for less here. Don't opt for a one-ring ceremony just to save some money. Don't accept a ring you don't feel good about simply because it's under a certain price. Just find the best price for what you really want. This is one of the most important elements of your wedding; in fact, it's the only thing you'll keep close to you day after day, so don't scrimp here.

Where to Find Your Rings

Look in magazines or brochures to get an idea of the kinds of rings you want. It's best to have a general idea when you walk into a jewelry store so you're not swayed by the extra-flashy choices in the display cabinet or by the commission-motivated salesclerk.

Before you start your hunt, do some research on what to look for in quality gold and precious gem jewelry. Diamonds, for instance, are priced according to carat, color, clarity, and cut. You'll want to know which specifications of each warrant the higher prices. Bridal magazines often run articles on how to buy a diamond, and you can get literature on the subject from a good jewelry store.

Bring along a relative or friend who knows something about jewelry when you're shopping. You'll be more likely to ask the right questions.

Ring stores in the mall may at times offer competitive prices during sales; in general, though, their prices will figure in location rental and upkeep fees. Their prime spot in the mall could mean less savings on retail prices.

Go to your family's regular jeweler for proven reliability and a possible discount for your loyalty to the place. One bride received 10 percent off on her rings just because she'd recently bought a gift there for her mother.

Comparison shop for your rings in different stores of different sizes, in different parts of town. Price tags do vary, and you may be able to find yourself a great deal.

Check discount jewelry stores and department stores. Sales fliers will announce special savings, and throughout-the-store discounts may apply at the jewelry counter.

If you have a friend in the business, see if you can use his or her employee discount to garner a better price for your rings. This of course takes a good friend, who will be giving up a slice of commission on your purchase. It's worth a shot.

Keep an eye out for sales, clearances, and specials. Ask your family and bridal party to watch for specials in stores near them as well. It could mean savings of 10 percent or more, which could translate into a sizeable discount.

Ask your friends and family for referrals to the stores where they bought their own rings.

If the store isn't a large one, part of a national chain or well-known line, check it out with the Better Business Bureau to see if it's legitimate or if any charges have been leveled against it. A ring purchase is a large-ticket item, so your best bet is to protect your investment— even before you make it.

Part of your criteria for choosing a ring shop is its engraving and sizing policies. If both are included free— and in some places they aren't—it's an advantage. Measure this one carefully, though, because an expensive store with free sizing and engraving is not better than an inexpensive store that charges extra for engraving and sizing.

Consider buying your rings in an antique shop, where beautiful rings with some history are offered at lower prices. Just be sure to get the rings appraised immediately to be sure you've gotten your money's worth. You may even find that your fifty-dollar ring is actually a valuable piece of jewelry.

If you're considering buying your wedding ring from a catalog that offers a line of gold sets, be sure to add up shipping and handling costs and tax before you call that toll-free number with your credit card. It may turn out that you're not getting a bargain at all. Try:

For information on how to buy a ring:

Jewelers of America	800-497-1480
Service Merchandise	800-251-1212
JCPenney	800-222-6161
Sears	800-473-7247

Jewelry Companies

ArtCarved	800-525-4985
Hamilton (platinum)	800-5HAMILTON
I Do Collection	800-622-8345, ext. 0326
La Marje	800-444-0507
Novell (platinum)	800-622-8345, ext. 0327
Joan Rivers Style	800-848-1055

Silver is less expensive than gold, and silver bands are gaining in popularity.

If you're ordering your rings from a catalog, make use of that little ring-sizing strip of paper most books include with the order form. You may wear a size six ring, but this company's sizes may be much larger or smaller than the norm. So take the measurement first and save yourself the cost of having to mail back your ring for a reorder. Since you're ordering from a catalog a ring you haven't tried on, make sure the catalog has a good return policy, and insure the package if you have to send it back.

No matter where you're ordering your rings, the choices you make can save you some money. Choose a set of plain rings over the swirly, gaudy ones that are larger than your whole hand . . . for obvious reasons. Another plus for smaller, simpler rings without texture and braiding is that they have no ridges to catch dirt, so they're easier to keep clean.

Buy plain gold bands rather than the kinds with the set stones.

Make sure you're getting your money's worth. Check the inside of the bands for a fourteen-carat ("14k") gold marking if that's what you're buying.

Less costly than silver and gold are jade and coral. Consider these novel ideas for unique bands . . . for you if not for him.

Economical choices may be gold- or silver-plated bands. They still carry the same meaning, no matter what they're made of.

Compare the prices of his and hers wedding band sets to the prices of individual rings. Only in that way can you decide which is the better buy. Some sets on sale can save you up to a hundred dollars off the price of individual rings.

If you know someone who makes jewelry as a hobby, commission that person to make your rings for you. No doubt the cost will be much lower than a store's, and your friend will be given a great honor. You also may design your own rings. Jillian, a recent bride, found it special to actually help create her and her husband's wedding bands. She designed the rings, then helped a friend make them. In doing so, she saved two hundred fifty dollars.

Put up fliers at a local art school or college with a jewelry workshop regarding your search for an artist to make a set of wedding rings. Students love these opportunities for their portfolios and independent study projects, and you'll undoubtedly get the ring for little more than the cost of materials. That can be more than half off store prices.

Look into the talents and prices of local crafters for custom-made rings at discount prices. Comparison shop among these artists as well.

For the ultimate savings and meaning, exchange rings handed down to you by relatives. Keeping the bands in the family is important, and it's a special tie to those who have worn the bands before you.

Have the stones from an heirloom ring set in your wedding band. You save money on them, and the inclusion of your grandmother's diamonds in your ring is a very special gesture.

Buy stones separately from a discount supplier, then have them set into a ring you've gotten a bargain on elsewhere. The savings here: fifty to two hundred dollars.

Don't fall for those too-good-to-be-true ring sales in odd locations—like the back of a van. And skip the cubic zirconias.

Payment

Get a written appraisal of your rings with your receipt.

Make sure your ring supplier offers a good return policy, in case you must exchange them for another size or style.

A good warranty should be offered to you as well. Ask about it.

Think seriously about whether you want to arrange an installment plan for paying off your rings. Interest will pile up, costing you much more money than the price of the ring. A better alternative is to use your credit card—ensuring you proper reimbursement in case of a problem and, at times, credits or frequent flyer miles. Just be sure to pay off that amount on your credit card with some of your wedding gift money so you're not accumulating interest due on your credit account.

After the Purchase

After you buy your rings, have them appraised immediately. Go to a jeweler other than the one from whom
you bought the ring for this service (why would the
salesclerk want you to know your ring isn't really worth
three hundred dollars?).

Have your rings insured immediately. In case of loss or
theft, you'll be reimbursed their full value.

Store your rings in a safe or lock box at home before the
wedding—just don't store them so safely away that you
forget where they are.

On the night before the wedding, leave a note on your
door not to forget the rings before you leave for the
ceremony!

22

Flowers and Decorations

Before you start looking for a florist, think about the items you'll want and need to order. Of course, you'll have your bouquet, your bridesmaids' flowers (another reason to have a smaller bridal party), boutonnieres, and some decorations, but how much do you really need to arrange?

Check with the officiant or the manager of the site of the wedding. Will the location be decorated already? If so, you have much less to buy. One bride learned that her church would be decorated already with poinsettias and white candles on the date of her pre-Christmas wedding. This saved her two hundred dollars in extra florist fees.

Another reason to check with the officiant at a church or synagogue is to inquire about rules regarding decoration. You may not be allowed to set up pew arrangements, and that would be an unfortunate thing to find out after you paid seventy-five dollars for yours. You should get the dos and don'ts before you start ordering.

See if there will be other weddings taking place at your wedding location on the same day as yours. Perhaps you could arrange through the officiant or manager to share basic decorations with the other bride or brides at a savings to all of you. Emily, a bride, asked the officiant to give her name to the other bride, who then contacted her. They saved two hundred dollars by splitting the costs of decorating their church.

Set a budget for your flowers, using the figures you've discovered through introductory research or talks with recently married friends, and stick to it.

Where to Look

Don't go to a big, fancy florist connected to a bridal salon, a mall, a hotel, or even a caterer. Their elevated prices mean you're also paying for their rent, their facilities, their advertising, and their larger staff. Instead, look at a more moderate supplier.

Use your family's regular florist, so that you're sure of their reliability and quality of service. You may even get a discount for being a regular customer. Karen, a bride, received a 20 percent discount on her wedding flowers from her regular florist, plus another 10 percent off because the same florist also did her sister's wedding.

Check wholesalers in your area. Their prices are by nature lower than those you'll find in other stores and markets. You'll find listings of these in your Yellow Pages.

Comparison shop in several different florists and nurseries in several different parts of town. Prices may vary depending on neighborhood, access, size of facilities, and type of clientele. Of course, suburban shops tend to be less expensive than urban ones, but the price of travel and transport could cancel out that discount, so search out the best areas at the least expense to you.

A shop that grows its flowers and plants on-site is generally less expensive than the shop that has to have all of its blooms shipped in. So look for greenhouse or gardening space around the shops you're checking out.

Ask your nearby friends and relatives if they would suggest a florist whose service they liked. Use that information when you're comparing prices and packages.

Find a young, just-starting-out-in-the-business person who will give his or her all. Most often, these beginners lack experience, not talent, and their reasonable prices are meant to attract accounts that will give them valuable exposure. Tracy, a bride-to-be, found a great new florist at considerable savings when a hardworking newcomer distributed fliers at the market. So don't count out the young ones. You might just get a great deal.

When comparison shopping at floral suppliers, look through their brochures and sample albums and ask to see arrangements they're working on now. Keep track of their prices and the elements of their packages so you can compare and contrast all the possibilities.

When ordering, keep several things in mind to save yourself some money:

Get a price comparison chart for each of the flowers you might want to include in your bouquets and decorations. This way, you'll be able to see which blooms are most and least expensive, and you can choose the most economical ones. Lilies, carnations, and freesia, for example, are far less costly choices than the popular stephanotis and orchids.

Use the florist's chart as well to find out which flowers have to be flown in. Shipping an exotic selection of flowers will be more expensive than those found closer.

> *My stephanotis had to be flown in from Hawaii. I paid over one hundred dollars for all of them. It's money we could have saved and used on our own trip to Hawaii.*
>
> *—Whitney, bride.*

Order flowers that are in season. Just like fruits and vegetables, prices go up when it's not their prime time.

Order the more popular flowers like carnations and baby roses. They're usually the least expensive and most appropriate choices.

Order miniature flowers rather than the full-sized variety. Not only are they more delicate, they may be priced at a fraction of the cost—depending on the particular flower.

Consider sprays, which have several flowers per sprig. One spray can give the appearance of several three-dollar flowers.

Use more greenery in your bouquets and decorations. The natural look is in, so include plenty of ferns and pretty leaves to fill out a bouquet with fewer flowers.

Consider filling out your bouquets and decorations with Queen Anne's lace or similar inexpensive blooms.

A more economical choice: Order the greenery such as the ferns and the fillers from the florist, but pick your own flowers from your garden. You can incorporate the flowers into your bouquet easily. Renée, a recent bride, saved an amazing six hundred dollars this way, and it was special for her to carry in her bouquet the flowers she and her fiancé had planted together.

Be sure the shape of your bouquet fits your height and size. A short bride looks hidden behind a too-large bouquet, so avoid ordering a more expensive style that isn't right for you.

❧

Carry long-stemmed roses tied with a pretty ribbon instead of a bouquet.

❧

Consider having your bridesmaids and maid of honor also carry long-stemmed roses tied with ribbon rather than a full bouquet.

❧

Order a much smaller bouquet as the one you'll toss to the waiting single women at your reception. There is no rule that says it has to be identical to your real one. Or you could just toss your own bouquet if you're not planning to preserve it and keep it as a memento of your day.

❧

Corsages to be worn by the mothers and grandmothers don't have to be very large. In fact, most women would prefer a smaller corsage to wear on the wedding day. Check if corsages worn on the wrist are less expensive than the pin-on variety at your floral designer's.

Rather than order flowered hairclips for your bridesmaids, plan to snip some baby's breath from bouquets or
even from your own garden to adorn their hair. Your
savings here, depending on the style, could reach a
hundred dollars.

To cut your florist's labor costs, simply order all the
flowers you'll need and make the bouquets, corsages,
boutonnieres, centerpieces, and pew decorations yourself. Check in your library for a how-to book, and visit
your discount craft supplier for florist wire and materials. Have a friend or a neighbor help with the flower
arranging and bouquet making. Check with your local
4H Club or Girl Scout organization for experienced
volunteers.

Before ordering a white aisle runner from your florist,
check to see if the church or wedding location has one of
its own, or simply skip the aisle runner. You'll look
better in contrast with a darker floor rather than the
white of the path. An off-white dress looks better, too,
without the white clash underfoot.

If your wedding location is nicely decorated already, you could skip the pew decorations. If your first several rows need to be reserved with some kind of markers, use lengths of ribbon instead.

Delivery

Bypass the delivery fee and pick up your order from the florist yourself. You could save twenty-five to fifty dollars, depending on the size of your order. Make sure you have plenty of insulated coolers and sturdy boxes so that all your flowers will arrive fresh and uncrushed at the wedding.

Of course, if you'll be picking up the flowers yourself, you'll want to arrange to do it at the last possible time before the ceremony. It could be a morning run after breakfast, or you could send someone from your bridal party in your place.

Decorating the ceremony and reception locations with these freshly picked-up supplies is another wedding morning task that might be best handled by a less-nervous bridal attendant or helpful friends and relatives.

Instead of contracting with a professional florist and staff to provide the flower arrangements and bouquets for your wedding, here are some frugal alternatives:

Do it all yourself, using flowers from your garden or from a relative or friend's garden or greenhouse and some instructions out of a how-to book from the library.

Start taking more cuttings from your plants and planting seeds way ahead of time so you'll have a good supply of flowers for your wedding. If you have the time, buy a ready-to-bloom rosebush, plant it, and collect your bouquet flowers when they're needed. One bride received a rosebush as an engagement present, and she was able to use her own roses, along with her other garden blooms at her wedding. She saved all of what would have been a four-hundred-dollar florist bill.

Visit a floral supply store for all tools and supplies you'll need to make boutonnieres, corsages, and pew decorations. Look in your Yellow Pages for a Rag Shop or Treasure Island. Again, look for instruction in craft books found in the library.

You can make your own chuppah (for your Jewish wedding) with flowers and garlands from your own garden. Again, consult how-to books, or just model your own after those you've seen.

Instead of ordering rose petals to be strewn about by the flower girl during the ceremony, gently pull the petals off several roses from your own garden. One bride who followed this tip saved $75 off her florist bill.

Another option for the flower girl is to provide her with confetti, which you can make with a hole punch and white paper or leftover bridal wrapping paper. Don't bother buying the fancy, shaped confettis now sold at party stores—it's not worth the expense.

5 bags store-bought confetti	$15
Homemade confetti	free

Use candelabras from your home. If you were to rent these for several tables, you could spend anywhere from twenty to fifty dollars.

If your wedding falls in the right season, cut evergreens from your Christmas tree (or from the discarded Christmas trees left on the curb by your neighbors) before you discard it. Unsold Christmas trees may be purchased after the season for a minimal price. Use the branches as centerpiece additions.

Use potted plants from home or borrow potted plants and flowering bushes from friends and family to decorate your reception.

Use dried flowers in your bouquet and as decorations. They look great at fall weddings, and you don't have to worry about wilting. Or use silk flower arrangements from your home.

Cut branches from flowering trees as decoration for your tables, buffet tables, and the altar. Again, this must be done very soon before the ceremony so your blooms aren't wilting and discoloring. Keep precut branches cool, and keep their angle-cut stems in water.

For a head table or buffet table, use your own good tablecloth from home rather than renting one.

Buy candles in bulk from discount stores, craft supply houses, even catalogs. And freeze them before using them—they'll last much longer.

Centerpieces

There's no need for those expensive florist-created centerpieces. Oversized ones obstruct your guests' view of one another (and you) anyway, and a pretty centerpiece doesn't necessarily have to have a price tag attached. Here are some inexpensive alternatives to the tabletop jungle:

Use small amounts of flowers you've picked from your own garden arranged in pretty vases you already own. Or borrow vases from friends and relatives if you have to.

Arrange candles of different heights and one color (white may be the least expensive) to create a romantic look for each table. Remember to freeze the candles first so they will burn more slowly.

Helium balloons rising a short distance above the center of each table offer a festive look. Not the least expensive option available to you, it is still a popular idea.

Set in the center of each table groups of framed pictures of you and your fiancé together, with family, with friends, as children, etc. Use the frames and pictures you've taken from your own walls and countertops, and recruit both families to bring theirs in as well. (Ask them to stick an address label on the backs of their frames for easier return after the party.) One bride found that her guests loved looking at the photos on the table; they were appreciated far more than one hundred dollars' worth of floral centerpieces would have been.

Float miniature candles along with flower petals in a large water-filled glass bowl at the center of each table. You can use your own—or borrow—large glass bowls, and then pick the flower petals from your backyard blooms. The cost here for a very classy look: under fifty dollars.

Arrange a fruit bowl at the center of each table or as a larger centerpiece of a buffet table. Search farmer's markets and supermarkets for the best quality and price available, or ask the reception hall manager if the fruit from the buffet table might be arranged this way.

A large bread basket makes a great centerpiece, especially if you include braided breads and a variation of shapes, sizes, and colors. Again, ask the caterer if you'd be able to use the bread intended for the buffet table for this purpose, or make the bread yourself. Use your own pretty baskets or borrow these as well. If baskets are not available to you, simply cover any kind of bowl with a large cloth napkin and have it drape over the bowl once it's filled with rolls. (In days long ago, grain was considered a symbol of fertility, and the bride and groom were showered with grain for that very reason. In other cultures of the past, bread was a gift brought by all and arranged in one pile. This is thought to be the origin of the wedding cake.)

Neatly arranged groups of wedding favors also make nice centerpieces. Why not get double duty out of your favors and save some money at the same time?

Check markets, sales, even your attic for items you can use as centerpieces. A brass theme will allow you to dig up all sorts of interesting things.

Other ideas if you're not the do-it-yourself type but you want the do-it-yourself savings:

Contact a floral design college or school to request their services as a group project for pay. The instructor will surely jump at your offer, and you'll wind up paying much less than you would to a commercial business. Quality is often outstanding, as these students are fresh in their knowledge of technique and the rules of design.

Accept the services of an experienced relative or friend as his or her wedding gift to you.

Contact your local florist or nursery to see if they might lend out larger trees and plants as decoration at your ceremony and reception. You never know.

Transportation for All

For the Bride and Groom

When dealing with limousines, always comparison shop. Prices vary *wildly*, and certain companies do offer special packages and discounts. Make plenty of calls and take plenty of notes. Of course, you'll need to know your wedding date when you start looking for a limo company—some agencies may not have any limousines available on your wedding day.

Never contract with a limousine agency just by phone. Always go to see the cars. You want to be sure you're not going to wind up with an old red model with a worn interior and no air conditioning—their version of "deluxe."

Contact the National Limousine Association at 800-NLA-7007 for resources and to check the track record of the limousine companies that interest you.

Ask what the drivers will be wearing. A reputable agency will have their drivers in suits or tuxedos.

When adding up the number of limousines needed, you can cut costs tremendously by just getting one for yourselves. The bridal party doesn't have to be transported in limos, after all.

Pass on the special bridal package that includes a complimentary bottle of champagne for the bride and groom. Most brides who paid for this type of package said either the champagne wasn't very good or the church and reception hall were so close that they didn't have any time to drink the champagne. Just a plain old ride in the car will do.

Be sure to schedule your time wisely. If you keep the limousine driver waiting outside the reception hall for you to leave the party—and you've stayed an hour longer than you planned to because you were having so much fun—you could wind up paying the driver for the extra time *plus* overtime. One bride and groom in this situation wound up paying the limo company two hundred dollars in extra fees. It's much smarter to keep the limo driver on call so that you can call his office to dispatch him when he's needed. Ask about time arrangements and extra fees.

Get a contract written up with all the details of your agreement, including the number of cars you'll need, where and when each of them is to report, deposits, and the signature or name of the person who took your reservation. Again, this is a larger expense, so you'll want to protect your investment. Plus, if one of the three limousines you've hired to transport the bridal party doesn't show up, you have proof that you're entitled to a partial refund.

If friends or relatives have special connections at a limousine company, ask if they might be able to get you a discount. Perhaps they could consider it their wedding present to you.

Limousines are not the only way to go. Look into alternative transportation:

Compare prices at car rental agencies—especially those that offer luxury or exotic cars. It might be cheaper to rent a convertible or even an Excalibur for an hour (to the ceremony and the reception only), rather than a limo.

Look in the Yellow Pages or in bridal magazines for special transportation such as horse and carriage rides. Research these carefully and always go to see the horse and the carriage. Consider here, though, the traffic in your area. Will this horse and carriage have to cross a four-lane highway to get to the reception?

Enlist the help of a friend with a nice car, possibly a convertible. With this free option, you're more likely to be able to decorate this car with streamers and "Just Married" signs than you are with a rented car or limousine.

Or use your own car. Just get a friend or relative—the best man or the maid of honor—to drive it.

If you live close to the ceremony and the reception, consider a walking procession from place to place. On a comfortable day, your parade will be great fun and the center of attention. Older or disabled guests can be driven the short distance, of course.

Have your parents or honor attendants drive you to and from the airport for your honeymoon. It's much smarter than hiring a limo, you don't have to worry about a waiting limousine driver and a ticking clock, and you get a better welcome home.

For the Bridal Party

Of course, limousines for the bridal party aren't a necessity, but if you do wish to provide them you should comparison shop among limousine companies. Since you'll be renting more than one limo, try for a group rate.

Figure out how many limousines you'll need before you start shopping. One is for you and the groom, obviously. Depending on how many bridesmaids and ushers are in your bridal party, you'll have to order more limousines.

Don't attempt to cram ten people into one limousine. Remember the women have dresses on that shouldn't be crushed and wrinkled by overcrowding in a car. Consider space while tallying cars.

Have helpful relatives and friends drive the bridal party around in their nice cars, cleaned, of course. Convertibles are fun for the celebrating group, so offer your car up as well if you have one.

The bridal party can drive themselves in a decorated minivan if one is available to them. Your parents', perhaps? Randi, a recent bride, was able to arrange minivan transportation for her bridal party. Not only was it a "party bus," as she called it, but it didn't cost her a dime. The van was her parents'.

After the reception, the bridal party may either be dropped off by a designated driver in his or her car, or if there will be no drinking, they can drive themselves home. A smart move would be to have the bridal party drop their cars off in the reception hall parking lot before the ceremony.

For the Guests

Before the wedding day, have the bridal party, friends, and relatives help transport out-of-town guests from the airport into town or to your house. No need to hire a shuttle or transport for them; this could cost you fifty to one hundred dollars depending on the number of guests coming in. You could pick them up yourself, but you might be too busy with final plans and fittings.

If many guests will be coming into town from far away, consider renting (or borrowing) a minivan to take them all from the hotel to the ceremony, to the reception, then back to the hotel at the end of the evening. This mass transit may be less expensive than shipping everyone in separate cars.

24

Music for the Ceremony

First, check with the wedding officiant about your plans for music during the ceremony. You don't want to hire a harpist for one hundred fifty dollars and then find out that the church does not allow outside performers or the secular music you've selected. Another reason to talk to the officiant: He or she may have several weddings to perform that day—all within tight time constraints—and your music may put your ceremony time over the limit. Unfair, I know. But it does happen. It's best to ask first.

Have as one of your criteria for choosing a wedding site the free service of the location's choir.

Remember, though, that the organist isn't always free. Tipping him or her is usually required.

If a relative, friend, or bridal party member is a professional musician, such as a harpist, pianist, or flutist, ask that person to perform at the ceremony as a wedding gift to you.

Ask your local high school or college choir to perform for a small fee, usually a donation to their upcoming trips and supplies fund. Some schools have specialty performing groups, such as madrigal choirs and even string quartets, as well.

Place an ad in a college newspaper for a harpist or flutist to perform at your wedding. No doubt you'll soon be flooded with calls from talented young people searching for experience, resume material, and a payment far below those expected by professional musicians. Anne, a bride, paid just twenty-five dollars for the harpist who performed at her wedding. It was the young harpist's first job, and Anne loved her music. A professional she called while researching musicians claimed a two-hundred-dollar fee. Just be sure to first listen to the performer you hire.

Rather than hiring a soloist, why don't you sing a song to the groom yourself? Or have him sing to you. (This only works if you have a bit more singing experience than just performing "My Girl" on the karaoke machine.)

If your wedding will be held outdoors, have some of your wedding music played over a good stereo sound system. You can get a tape of classical or designated wedding music for free in the library.

When choosing music to be played at your wedding, consider adding a wedding song from your heritage. Either give your choice of sheet music to the performer you've arranged, or once again get a cassette of that music free in your public library.

Or, for the biggest savings and not too large an effect on your ceremony, you could choose not to have a pianist, harpist, flutist, or choir perform a song during or before your wedding. The church organists, perhaps, could be allowed to play the processional, a hymn, and the recessional. It might be a bit boring, but it is traditional. Actually, not too many people will expect more than the standard organist, so you're off the hook if this is your choice.

> *It was very hot on the day of my August wedding. Everyone was glad we weren't having songs performed during the ceremony.*
>
> —*Lynn, bride.*

25

The Photographer and Videographer

Wedding photos and videos are too important to warrant big cost-cutting efforts. You get what you pay for here, so it's best to focus on smart shopping, getting more for the money you will spend.

The Photographer

If you're planning to hire a professional photographer, it's very important to comparison shop. Not only are you looking for the best prices and the best packages, you're also looking at the photographers' samples and the quality of their work. Are they dependable? Do they offer extras? Keep track of each photography service you consider so that you may narrow down the field later and choose from the best.

Ask a recently married friend if she'd recommended her photographer. If she raves about his or her work and has attractive albums and portraits to support the glowing review, your search for quality has landed on a target. If the price is right, this photographer is a good choice.

Note that membership in the Professional Photographer's Association of America, listed on a business card, means the photographer is well trained. It's a good way to check credentials.

When looking through photographers' sample albums and photographs, look not only for focus and a pretty subject (they'll of course show you only their best work) but for pictures taken in different lighting and different settings, a variation of vertical and horizontal, more candid than stiff posed shots, special lenses, and whatever other ideas you have for your own album. You'll want to be sure you're getting every penny's worth when you hand over what could be a pretty hefty check.

A quick check with the Better Business Bureau can reveal if any of your final choices for photographer have had any charges or complaints against them. You should know of your photographer's and videographer's past records if you're to trust them with such an important event.

A less costly option would be to hire the photographer only for the ceremony and the beginning of your reception. After all, these are the most important times to capture. There would be no need to keep the photographer on for the full five hours of the reception . . . particularly if your guests have cameras of their own. You can always get prints of their candid dancing scenes. One bride saved five hundred dollars with this option, and she noticed no difference in the quality of the photos from her reception.

Go through the photographers' lists of available packages. What is the minimum number of pictures you will need? Do you really need one thousand regular prints, twelve eight-by-tens, thirty four-by-fives, and one hundred wallets? You can save a lot of money by ordering just the number of pictures you'll need—both to keep for yourself and to give as gifts.

If the photographer's package offers you the full set of proofs to keep for free, you're getting a nice stack of pictures that you would have had to pay for otherwise.

> *We were allowed to keep all of our proofs. That was about two hundred fifty dollars' worth of pictures we didn't have to order.*
>
> *—Jean, bride.*

Don't be pressured into ordering special photo albums from the photographer for parents, grandparents, the bridal party, and others. For half the price of this service you can make your own albums with extra copies of your pictures (perhaps some of the proofs or pictures taken with your own camera) and inexpensive store-bought photo albums. You may even do your own wedding album using the professional pictures and a book you've purchased from the store. It all adds up to great savings if you do a good enough job arranging the pictures in the albums.

Don't be pressured into ordering special photo albums for people you don't like. It sounds harsh, but your parents will undoubtedly attempt to push some of their wishes on you throughout the planning of the wedding. This is usually one of them. If Mom wants mean Aunt Bertha to have some pictures, let Mom pay for it.

Another money-saving approach to the photographer's package is to order a percentage of your pictures in black and white. It may be cheaper, depending on your photographer, and these shots look very elegant. Besides, these pictures will not fade as quickly as color prints will. Check price comparisons carefully.

Some brides choose to skip the professional bridal portrait, usually taken several weeks before the wedding.

> *It's just an extra expense to me. I had four thousand portrait-posed pictures taken of me on my wedding day as part of the package, so why would I want to pay an additional fee for one more?*
>
> —Carol, bride.

Skip the gimmick shots. Do you really need to pay extra for a picture of the two of you superimposed over the sheet music of "your song"? While it might be a fun memento, it's also a nonessential.

Or consider this arrangement: The professional takes the pictures and you have them developed. This only works if you can find a real bargain on the development. If you trust yourself and if you have a great deal of experience, you could save a bundle by developing your photos at home with your own equipment. Or have a friend help.

Get a copy of the contract, just to clarify the specifics of your agreement and the package you've chosen, and keep your payment receipts in case any questions arise.

While many brides consider the wedding pictures too important to be left to an amateur, you may weigh your options differently. A friend or relative with plenty of photography experience can do just as wonderful a job as a pro, and he or she has the added advantage of knowing your guests and knowing what pictures you'll really want. Plus, you won't be charged anywhere near the fee of a professional photographer. If your friend will lend his or her picture-snapping services for free as a wedding gift to you, you should supply him or her with more than enough film to last through the ceremony, reception, and post-reception events. But don't look for cheap film to cut costs here. You want to get the best film you can. Just remember how much you're already saving by not hiring a photographer. Of course you'll pay for developing the film yourself, so keep this in mind when you buy your film—consider how many pictures you'll really need, then buy accordingly.

Have two friends take pictures at the ceremony. Both could work the ceremony, providing different perspectives, and they could then take turns capturing special moments of the reception.

> *This way, my friends helped me out by saving me one thousand dollars but neither of them had to work all night.*
>
> —*Marie, bride.*

Buy film with more exposures per roll. This usually is the most economical way to go, although you should always check prices.

Have your volunteers use their own cameras so they don't have to learn the intricacies of someone else's during the ceremony. This is no time for trial and error. If, however, you have an outstanding camera and would prefer to use it for the wedding photos, give the camera to your volunteer a week or two before the wedding with a roll or two of film—just so he or she can get the hang of using it. Saving money usually means taking extra care to prevent the worst.

Tell your friend to take several shots of the major parts of the ceremony and reception so you won't lose all record of your first kiss if the one picture of it didn't come out. Several shots will be your insurance.

Many brides are choosing to put one of those throwaway cameras on each table at the reception. Guests then take candid shots of you, themselves, and all the dancing and fun going on around you. While you're dancing your first dance, Cousin Fred may be taking his cue to propose to his girlfriend . . . finally. Moments like these don't have to get away. Just make sure you don't overspend on those throwaway cameras. Each one will cost you anywhere from eight to fifteen dollars, depending on where you shop—plus developing. If you figure the costs wisely, you can still do this and cut your wedding picture spending.

When comparison shopping for picture developing, consider that on-site developing may turn out to be less expensive. Investigate the numbers.

Do not go to one of those one-hour developing places just because you can't wait to see your wedding photos. You'll just wind up paying extra for the convenience. Save some money and wait those few days.

If you'll be turning in eighty rolls of film, see if you can negotiate for a lower, bulk developing price. You may get 5 or 10 percent off. It adds up.

When considering mail-away developing, don't forget the price of postage. Some brides would be too nervous to trust their pictures to the mail system, but discounted prices can make this worth the risk and effort.

Rather than order a wedding photo album from a bridal catalog or a store, simply use a regular, plain photo album without the fancy lettering. You can decorate your own album with fabric and lace for a personal touch.

Store-bought wedding photo album	$40
Homemade wedding photo album	$15–$20

The Videographer

Ask a friend if she'd recommend hers, then take a look at her wedding video to see if it's the sort you would like. This is the best way to be sure you're getting your money's worth.

Comparison shop, again not only for price but for packages and quality. Look at the videographer's samples— the full-length ones, not the snippets of his or her best work. Look for focus, good lens work, graphics, smooth transitions, even soundtrack.

Ask the videographer about his or her style. You don't want the video camera in your face all night, so make sure the videographer can get the footage without being underfoot. And ask what he or she wears to weddings. A suit? Tuxedo? Make sure this person will dress appropriately—this is *your* wedding.

Choose your video package carefully. How much time do you really think you'll need? Do you want to spend the money for film of you getting ready in the morning? How many copies do you really need?

As with everything having to do with your planning, get a copy of your contract as a record of your agreement, complete with specific details and the videographer's signature or name. Keep all receipts as proof of payment.

Do you really need a video? The professional videographer is the first service to be cut by most brides. At over seven hundred dollars in most cases, it is a nonessential compared with most other things.

Have two or three different friends tape your wedding and reception with their own video cameras from different angles. A good editing job will give your tape a professional look.

Professional videographer	$500–$1,500
Friends helping out	free

Of course, you'll supply the videotapes for your volunteer videographers. Again, don't buy cheap tapes, or the quality of the picture and sound will reflect the price you paid. Instead, spend the money for quality equipment.

Don't buy too many tapes. Look instead for long-running tapes and allow yourself several. Figure out the amount of time you'll have to cover before shopping, and get a bit more than that. If the amount of time warrants it, arrange to buy your tapes in bulk.

If your videographer will be using your video camera, give it to him or her a few days before the wedding to get used to it and its functions. Teach your friend how to use it. Point out fade-in, scanning, zooming, speed of movement, etc. Then view together the practice filming.

Discuss where the videographers will be set up during the ceremony and reception. It's a good idea to bring these volunteers to the rehearsal so that they can map out their positioning and instructions, as well as to note any restrictions for your wedding location.

Set up a system whereby your volunteer videographer can easily keep track of which tapes are used and unused throughout the wedding day—perhaps a sticker or a different case for full tapes. You don't want a confused camera operator to record over your vows to get the throwing of the garter.

When you have the tapes, arrange your own fancy editing. Either do it yourself or ask a talented friend to help. Professional videographers aren't the only ones who can create an introduction filled with your old baby pictures and stills of the two of you during your dating years.

> *I figured we saved one hundred fifty dollars by editing and recording our own baby pictures and through-the-years footage, and a pro couldn't have done it better.*
>
> —*Kathy, bride.*

Borrow one of those home-movie-to-video transformers—the kind that also allows you take film of slides and prints—to make your own special introductory sequence. Borrow another idea of the professional videographer: Add in some interview footage of you and your husband talking about your relationship, the wedding, each other. For many brides, this is the kind of special extra that they believe makes it worthwhile to spend two thousand dollars on a videographer alone. If only they knew they could do it all themselves, they'd save as much money as you can.

If you're planning to make copies of your wedding video for family and friends, copy your master tape onto a quality videotape, and then use that copy to make all the other copies. You don't want to put too much strain on your master tape. After all, you'll be viewing it yourself many times.

After the wedding, thank your friends and relatives who acted as photographers and videographer with nice gifts and notes of your gratitude. Their kindness and willingness to help has not only saved you a great deal of money, they've given you a priceless gift you'll undoubtedly cherish forever.

26

Wedding Programs

The wedding program is an outline of your wedding service and a roster of the bridal party, officiant, and other notable people taking part in your ceremony. These are most often decorative, with poems, pictures, and a personal note from the bride and groom. They're a nice touch and a wonderful memento.

Instead of ordering plain programs from the bridal stationery store or catalog—usually the same place you've ordered your invitations—make your own. With a quality computer, your options are endless, and you have creative control over the process.

| Store-bought programs | $50–$75 |
| Homemade programs | $10–$30 |

Look first at examples of wedding programs, either the ones from your cousins' weddings or those featured in bridal magazines. Aside from their format, what special additions would you like for your own?

Draw up your program, with precise wording and an idea of your layout. You'll need to know how many pages your program will be in order to figure copying costs. Of course, if you can fit your program on four sides (the fronts and backs of each side of a folded paper) you'll only need one sheet of paper for each program.

Either write up the program yourself in neat calligraphy, have a talented friend do it, or find an art student to do the calligraphy for you. Perhaps if you've hired one to do your invitations, you could have him or her do the program as well. Look back in the Invitations section for more advice about hiring someone to do the calligraphy for you.

If you like the look of calligraphy but don't trust your hand at it, use the calligraphy font on your home computer. You'll get flawless letters along with a neat page setup and (depending on your program) the ability to view the page on the screen without having to print it out first. There's no better way to save money on a professional-looking, personal job.

What if you don't have a computer with which to make a master copy? Use a friend's, a relative's, the library's, or the one at work. It's not too tough to find a computer to use for free nowadays.

Save even more money by printing out every copy of your program on your own computer. Use quality white paper or parchment bought by the pound or in bulk at any discount or stationery store.

If your printer isn't top quality and your computer ink and paper are expensive, see if you can beat those costs by taking your master copy to a discount printer. Depending on the paper you choose, the total cost may be diminished, and the results look great.

A decorative cover for your program is always a nice touch. Look in stationery stores and religious bookstores to find a good selection of program covers, and comparison shop. They're not very expensive at all, but you do want to get the best prices you can.

Instead, have an artist friend or relative design and create program covers for you. Again, it could be a gift, and it's a nice personal touch.

Store-bought program covers	$25–$50
Homemade program covers	$5–$10

See if your printer will collate your programs and program covers, then bind them at the crease. Many places will do this for free. If not, simply fold each one and slip the program inside the cover unattached.

Unfortunately, as nice as they are, programs may also be seen as nonessentials and cut from the wedding plans. You can live without them.

27

The Guest Book

Don't buy one of those fancy, plumey, overpriced guest registry books in the bridal salon or in a bridal supply catalog. Instead, get a plain one at a discount stationery store. A white cover that says nothing is every bit as classy and appropriate as the kind with the shiny gold lettering and picture.

A wedding guest book is a great gift idea from the flower girl and ring bearer or other member of the wedding party.

Forget the frilly feather pen that usually comes with those bridal guest book sets. A plain gold or white one you already own will do just as well.

Make your own personalized guest book from a plain, unused journal, or designate the back pages of your own personal wedding journal for the signatures and messages of your guest.

> *I saved twenty dollars by using my journal for my guests' register. And it was nice to have the one book as a complete keepsake.*
>
> —*Tara, bride.*

Appoint someone to be in charge of taking the guest book to the ceremony location, to the reception, and back home afterward. You don't want the book to be misplaced.

28

Decorating
the Reception Location

*For the ultimate in savings and ease, the location you've chosen
may already be decorated, so your additions may be minimal.
But in many cases you'll have to provide the materials and the
work. Before you start looking for decorations, consider whether
or not a theme wedding is right for you. If so, you'll have a
better idea of where to look for the things you need. Here are a
few general decorating tips:*

Regular balloons are less expensive than helium-filled
ones.

Plain balloons are less expensive than the shiny, mylar ones, and bunches of these are every bit as festive as the fancier selections.

❧

White balloons may be less expensive than colored ones, depending on where you're shopping.

❧

Borrow an air compressor to blow up the balloons, or rent a helium tank and buy your own balloons on sale at a party store. Shop around for the best buys.

❧

Plain crepe paper isn't the most glamorous of decorations, but with a lot of work it can look very good. Practice ahead of time.

❧

Use strings of white Christmas lights you already own to adorn trees or the ceiling in a dimly lit room.

> *By using our own Christmas lights in the room, we created a classy look for free.*
>
> —*Wendy, bride.*

❧

Borrow white or colored Christmas lights from your family and friends to decorate a larger or outdoor setting for next to nothing.

Decorate the walls and buffet table with silver-framed pictures of you and your husband, your parents and siblings at their weddings, your husband's relatives at their weddings. This is a favorite of many brides today. It's a touching tribute to special relatives, and it's virtually free.

Decorate a ceiling or gazebo roof with mobiles you can make yourself. Choose from hearts, sparkles, crystals, stars, whatever you'd like. If you question the idea of mobiles, just hang straight lines with decorations at the ends. The result is your own starry sky.

Commission an artist or a culinary institute student to make an ice sculpture for you. Put an ad on the bulletin boards at a nearby school announcing your need for a sculptor. You may be able to arrange for a sculpture at a price of around fifty dollars or even less, depending on the size and complexity.

Rather than renting a trellis, use the one that's already set up in your yard or at the reception location. Have a handy relative or friend make one using wood from a discount supply store.

Borrow a friend's, relative's, or neighbor's trellis.

Check out theme party books in your library to find ideas for your theme wedding. You don't need a party planner for this.

With a theme wedding, use the items you have handy. For example, if you're planning a Mexican fiesta wedding, plan to use your brother's souvenir sombrero as one of the decorations. Use your patterned rugs and throws as well. If you rented these items and others like them, you'd pay up to one hundred fifty dollars easily.

If you don't own it, see if you can borrow it. If you can't borrow it, see if you can make it. If you just can't make it, rent it.

At the very least, play up the natural attractions of the reception location. If there's a lovely view of the sunset, for example, part of the atmosphere is already set. Minimal decor is needed otherwise. So try to see your location at the time of day when your party will be taking place so you can get a look at the natural lighting and features.

29

Planning the Menu

Since the food is a major part of the reception, and the reception a major part of the entire wedding, you'll probably find this area too important to sacrifice much in the name of saving money. You want the food to be good, so don't plan on cutting costs to the point of its quality suffering.

If you'll be having the reception catered by professionals:

Before you can contract a caterer, you'll need to know exactly what kind of reception you'll be having—the level of formality, the theme, the location, time of day. As mentioned previously, an earlier wedding is a less formal one and is therefore less expensive because you will not be serving a full sit-down dinner. An afternoon wedding means you'll most likely be serving only hors d'oeuvres and cake and coffee. An early evening wedding, before eight o'clock, usually includes that full dinner or buffet, and an after-eight reception is often served by hors d'oeuvres and cake again. So obviously you'll need to know what kind of package and menu you're looking for before you can settle on a caterer.

Do your research to compare the caterers available to you. Compare general costs, of course, along with other package elements such as equipment, linens, cleanup, and the like. Keep track of your notes and comparisons so that you can narrow the choices down when you're ready to make your final decision.

Ask a recently married friend or relative if she'd recommend the caterer who did her reception. If you remember the food at her reception as particularly outstanding and the service as exemplary, then you'll be able to make your choice based on experience. Several brides report savings of 10 to 15 percent as referrals from previous customers. Caterers depend on word-of-mouth advertisement, and you could profit.

When you're researching caterers, do your introductory work over the phone, but always go to the business in person for the next step. You'll want to see their samples, their linens and china if that's part of their package, and their overall appearance as a successful business. While there, see if you can arrange to taste their menu selections. Many caterers expect this request as part of today's smart wedding shopping, and they keep a supply of hors d'oeuvres on hand.

Ask for references, then use them. Place a call to several of their recent clients and—knowing that, of course, only people who were happy with their work will be referred to you—ask about the good qualities of the caterer's service.

A good standard by which to measure possible caterers is their membership in the International Food Service Executive Association. Membership in this organization listed on the company's business card means the caterer is well trained and has met the requirements of the association.

The Better Business Bureau can tell you if any charges or complaints have been registered against the caterers you're researching. A good history in the business is a positive indication of their reliability, whereas a negative mark could make you think twice about investing in that business's services. After all, it's your wedding.

Use your best instincts when researching caterers. Are they forthcoming with information? Do they seem willing to go by your wishes, or do they seem to want to be in control? Do they seem organized? Do you feel comfortable with them?

When you've settled on a caterer, choose your menu carefully. The courses and foods you choose will undoubtedly affect the price you're paying, so follow these hints from brides who have been there:

Choose a menu that is right for the season of your wedding. Some heavier foods should not be served in the summer.

Ask for a price list for each type of entree or appetizer. Your caterer should be able to provide you with this information so you can tell at a glance which choices are less expensive.

> *The price list allowed me to compare the Brie tartlets with the coconut shrimp and the mini quiches. As a result, I was able to save one hundred and seventy-five dollars with my choices.*
>
> *—Anna, bride.*

Choose more popular, simpler foods. Exotic choices mean more money.

Skip the big cheese-cube tray during the cocktail hour. It will hardly be touched if you're offering other selections, and it can go bad if left out too long.

Don't plan on having a seafood bar or other specialty food bar set up at the reception if other food will be served. While the choice may be appetizing, it's a nonessential. An *expensive* nonessential.

Avoid obviously expensive foods such as caviar and lobster tails.

For the entree, have the caterer offer your guests a choice of a meat or a nonmeat entree. Not only will this probably lower the price quoted in your contract, you'll please your health-conscious guests.

> *Just by choosing chicken and stuffed shells as choices over chicken and filet mignon, we saved ten dollars per guest. That's fifteen hundred dollars.*
> —*Marianne, bride.*

Do you really need several different kinds of vegetables? Cut down the list and save some money. Everyone's going to be saving room for the cake anyway.

Forget the extra dessert trays and the chocolate mousse. Let them eat cake. Savings here could reach ten dollars per guest.

Skip the international coffee bar. Order instead plain and decaffeinated coffee.

The manner in which the food is served may also affect the caterer's final bill. Appetizers served butler-style are very nice, but it may be less expensive to have the appetizers arranged on several tables around the room. Buffet style for a less formal reception may be a more economical choice than paying for servers.

Or arrange a more economical deal with your caterer. Have them prepare the food, and you do the rest. You pick it up, you set it up, you clean it up.

Or along the same lines, only contract for half of the meal to be catered. The caterer does the entree, and you do the appetizers and desserts.

Don't go for expensive food decorations and displays. You don't need a shrimp cocktail sculpture in the shape of a three-dimensional heart, do you? Believe it or not, you could wind up paying up to a hundred fifty dollars for a food sculpture like this.

Arrange for some members of your bridal party and perhaps some relatives and friends to help out in the kitchen a few days before the wedding.

Get a copy of the contract, including a full, in-detail listing of the package and menu you're purchasing from them. As an added precaution, get the name of the person who took your order, and write down the date and time it was taken. Keep all payment receipts and perhaps even a copy of your check, in case of conflict over the bill later on.

> *The caterer swore that I had one more payment to make, when I was sure I had already paid it in cash. Basically, she won, and I had to pay her another two hundred fifty dollars.*
> —*Bonnie, bride.*

If you'll be catering the reception yourself:

Use the menus you've found in the caterers' brochures to plan your own appetizers and entrees. You'll find you can plan and serve identical meals for a fraction of caterers' prices.

Plan your menu around popular, inexpensive foods.

Use your own favorite recipes, or get recipes from cookbooks free in the public library.

If you'd like to serve some ethnic foods at your reception, check with your local heritage organization. They may be able to help you with recipes, pricing, and even their own frozen selections. One bride received a big 30 percent discount and some help in the kitchen from her heritage association's expert cooks.

Borrow the extra equipment you'll need, such as baking pans, stockpots, etc. No need to rent them.

Shop in bulk. Check wholesale markets for the ingredients you'll need.

When pricing food and supplies, always shop by unit prices. You can always discover hidden bargains that way.

Buy foods that are in season—they're less expensive.

If you're in the military, use your commissary privileges for great savings on your food and liquor. One military bride estimated her savings at the commissary to total three hundred fifty dollars. Tax-free items add up in savings.

Always try a new recipe months in advance so you don't find out too late that it doesn't work or tastes terrible.

Plan to buy trays of specialty food from your local deli or the take-out section at the caterer's. Just transfer the Swedish meatballs and bacon-wrapped Brie onto serving plates, and you have catered quality for a near home-made price.

Garnish plates of your appetizers to give them a professional look. Your guests will never know.

Decorate the appetizer table with flowers and framed pictures so that the full table makes it look like there's more food.

Volunteer helpers can set up, serve, and clean up. Good people to ask are friends of your younger brother (he'll have a better time if they're there) and your friends' children.

Make use of your warehouse club membership, or go as a guest on a friend's membership.

Beverages

For some brides, the idea of an open bar goes without saying. Their families would expect no less, and they'd consider a cash bar to be an attack on their station in life. So instead of canceling the open bar and risking the wrath of your relatives, choose instead to limit the choices offered at that open bar. Have the bartender offer a smaller range of wines, mixed drinks, and soft drinks instead of opening the place's full stock to your guests.

❧

Choose to serve nonalcoholic drinks only. Punch stretches out a long way. Add some champagne for taste and fizz.

Close the bar early. Not only will you save some money, but your guests will have more time to dance off their champagne before having to leave.

> *We negotiated one hundred dollars off our reception hall bill by arranging to close the bar one hour before the end of our reception. The manager totaled up drink prices per guest, and we got a discount.*
> —*Katie, bride.*

Provide your own alcohol and drink mixes rather than go by the reception hall's prices. Surely you can find a less expensive wine cooler.

Check first to see if your location has any liquor restrictions. If you find out too late that it doesn't have a liquor license, you won't be able to use your supplies. That's hundreds of dollars wasted.

If your reception location requires you to use their liquor at their prices, negotiate as best you can with the manager. Can you offer only part of their stock to your guests? Can you be reimbursed for unopened bottles?

If you're given the choice, arrange to serve only the less expensive brands of beer and wine. Research several months before the wedding to find your best picks and best prices.

Shop again for liquors in your warehouse club or in your military Class Six store.

Choose punch for the kids instead of soft drinks.

You don't have to skip the champagne toast just to save some money. Look around for a good domestic champagne, and remember that a cheap bottle of champagne is definitely a cheap bottle of champagne. Sample some choices yourself or ask a friend what she served at her reception.

Arrange to provide only one glass of champagne per guest—just for the toast. You'll limit your needs to only eight or ten bottles of champagne, rather than twenty or thirty.

Instead of champagne, toast with other drinks. It's the toast itself that counts.

Speaking of champagne, you'll need bride and groom toasting flutes. As always, don't just plan on buying the ones in the bridal salon or the bridal catalog. Instead, get pretty plain champagne flutes at a regular department store and tie a satin ribbon around the stem. Or designate the toasting flutes as the maid of honor's wedding gift to you. Or the best man's, or the bridal party's, or your best friend's.

Make a lot of ice, more than you'll need, and store it all in trash bags in your extra freezer. Fill bundt cake pans with water and freeze those for pretty floats for the punch bowl.

Or check with a restaurateur or hotelier friend. He or she might let you use the industrial ice machines at little cost.

31

Reception Entertainment

When shopping around for musical performers or a DJ
for your reception, consider which of the two you'd like.
Both have pros and cons. A band can personalize songs
for you, whereas a DJ plays "the real thing" and doesn't
go on so many breaks. With that in mind, investigate
whichever kind of musical source you've chosen.

Next, consider the type of music you want. Classical,
pop—the performer you choose should have a broad
repertoire. A band's inability to play the kind of music
you like narrows the field of possibilities by one.

Compare packages. What can each DJ or each band offer you? When you compare specifics, you'll get a better idea of what your money will be getting you.

A major factor in choosing the entertainment is the amount of space you'll have available for them. A band works well in a spacious reception hall with a stage, but a wedding at home or in a smaller room creates limitations on your choice. A DJ or soloist is perhaps the better selection for these.

Consider the facilities of your reception location. Level ground is needed for DJs and most bands, and it's best to make sure your location has enough electrical outlets and power. An unforeseen problem means you could lose your entertainment at the last minute, along with the three hundred dollars you paid for it.

Consider your crowd when searching for a DJ or band. If your guests will be of the older set, you'll want to provide music they'll appreciate. The same goes for your younger guests. So arrange music according to what your guests will actually dance to. The type of music will determine the kind of band or DJ you'll get.

If you're having trouble deciding between the two, treat them as equals when you're comparison shopping and just go for the better prices and packages.

Compare prices per hour versus flat fees, and figure out how many hours you think your reception will last. Ask your recently married friend how long her reception was and whether or not she wanted to add on a few more hours at the end.

Find out what the fees are for adding extra hours at the end of the evening. Your whole group may be having so much fun at the reception that you decide to ask the DJ or band to stay on for one more hour. What are the extra charges for doing so, or is it just another hourly rate? It's important to know this ahead of time, as a decision made at the actual reception could cost you a small fortune in additional fees.

Get recommendations from recently married friends, or just hire a group you've already seen at another wedding.

Ask if you can view a video of the DJ's work. Most professionals provide this service.

Better yet, if you're going to hire a band, go hear them at an actual reception if you can. No one will mind if you step in to listen for a moment.

If you're checking out DJs, find out what he or she will be wearing to the reception. State your preference for a suit or tuxedo if the DJ will be a man, or a dress or tuxedo if it will be a woman.

Specify how many breaks the band will be allowed to take during the reception. You won't want to pay them for five hours of playing when they've really only played for three.

> *We learned the hard way. We paid for four hours of music, and the band took so many breaks—one after every three or so songs—we estimated they only played for two. So basically their hourly rate was doubled for actual work done.*
>
> *—Tricia, bride.*

Draw up a contract, and get signatures for verification. Record the date and time of the contract as well.

As an added precaution—and this comes from a bride who learned a lesson the hard way—specify the kind of music the band will be playing and all of the band members' names.

> *When I contracted a band from my home town, they were a pop group. Four men and a woman. I liked their Motown selections and their romantic ensembles. But when they showed up at my reception, the band had changed members and focus. So I had six men performing Euro-club tunes. It was completely inappropriate for my reception.*
>
> *—Kelly, bride.*

To avoid the same problem, recognize that bands may change lead singers and selection during the six months between the contract and the wedding. Keep in contact with the band—just tell them you're confirming again— and make sure your contract lets you out of the agreement without monetary obligation if the band should change. (This, by the way, is a reason why DJs are so popular at weddings.)

Give the DJ or band you're hiring a list of songs you'd like to hear at your reception, including special numbers such as line dances and group numbers. Also give them a list of songs you *don't* want them to play. Some songs may remind you of other times, other places, and other people, and you want to make sure they're not a part of your day.

Get a copy of your payment receipt and a copy of your check as proof of payment. Money questions later down the road can be silenced with good record keeping.

If a friend or a family member has a band or is a professional musician, let him or her play for a while, perhaps during the band's breaks. Of course, if your talented acquaintances would like the exposure of working your entire reception—and they sound good to you—try to arrange an amount you could pay them. If they refuse payment, offer them a free meal instead, or simply accept their performance as a gift. One bride arranged for her stepbrother's band to play at her wedding as his gift to her. The savings: six hundred fifty dollars she would have had to pay to a professional group.

Hire a college or high school musical group to perform at your reception. These young people studying to be professional musicians or instructors take their performances seriously, and you'll only have to pay them a fraction of what you'd pay an actual professional. If you've arranged for a school group to perform at your ceremony, ask them to work the reception, too. Tell them they can enjoy the party on their breaks.

Or just ask the person who performed at your ceremony to play a few hours at the reception as well. Using one person for both saves you time and money.

Have a friend of the family or a colleague from work act as DJ during your reception. Make sure he or she has experience with this sort of thing, then set up your own sound system and your favorite CDs, and let him or her go to work as a favor or gift to you.

Make your own music mixes for this volunteer DJ to play. Alternate fun songs with slow ones, traditional ethnic music with party classics, so that all your favorites are played at your reception.

If you're not a good music mixer, get CDs or tapes free from your public library. They'll have a wide range of party tapes, sixties music, and romantic collections for you to borrow.

Don't just turn on a cassette player in the corner of the room. See if the reception hall has a way of hooking your music up to their hidden sound system.

See if your reception hall is able to pipe into the room their own prerecorded classical music.

Or for a truly unique reception—not to mention a savings on the band fee—rent a jukebox that is filled with all your favorite songs. (Perhaps your reception location already has one set up in their party room.) Check with party rental stores, and be sure to ask for the titles of the songs programmed into the machine before you rent it. A jukebox that plays only old and out-of-date music might not fit the bill.

Dancing to the Music

You'll read in the bridal magazines, and friends will make the suggestion, to consider taking professional dancing lessons so that you'll look good out on the dance floor. But professional dance lessons, even adult courses given at night at the high school, cost money. Instead, rent a video on ballroom dancing. Teach your partner the basic steps he'll need to get through the spotlight dance and practice together for a while.

Enlist the aid of your light-footed parents or grandparents to help you both learn how to do a waltz or the cha-cha. Then, in turn, you can teach them how to do today's line dances. You'll all have lots of fun learning together and showing off your new skills at the party.

32

The Cake

Don't order your cake through your bridal salon. Some offer such services in their bridal packages, but you could wind up having to pay five hundred dollars for a simple three-tier cake.

You'll get a better price if you order your cake from a baker rather than a caterer. Only your comparison shopping can tell you for sure what the specifics are, of course, but this is a general prescript.

Use your family's regular bakery. You know they're reliable, you've tasted their cakes before, and you may just get a discount for being a regular customer. One bride recently received a 50 percent discount from her family's regular bakery.

> *It helped that I'm one in six daughters, and the bakery would love to do all of our family's weddings.*
>
> *—Danita, bride.*

Comparison shop at bakeries of different sizes, in different parts of town. Their prices will definitely vary, and you won't always get a better cake in a larger bakery.

When comparison shopping at bakeries you've never been to before, always ask if you can sample a piece of their wedding cakes. It's not as strange a request as it sounds, and it's the best way to be sure you're getting a good cake for your money.

Ask a recently married friend where she ordered her wedding cake, and get yours at the same place if the price is right.

If you'll be attending a wedding in the near future, make a note of the wedding cake, and ask the bride where she ordered it.

Does the bakery deliver the cake to the reception location for free, or is there a charge? Ask before you order.

When ordering your wedding cake, you'll have to tell the baker how many guests will be in attendance at your wedding. Take ten off your grand total, since not everyone eats cake at the reception. There are those who skip the cake because they're dieting, those on special medical orders not to have sweets, and those who are too busy dancing to sit down for a slice cake. The smaller number means you'll be paying that much less for your bakery-made cake. Just don't go too low—you wouldn't want to have guests left without a piece.

Ask for a copy of the order for your cake, checking twice to make sure the baker has recorded the right size, filling, icing, decorations, date of wedding, location of the reception, and phone number to reach you. A lost or wrong cake is one of the most common wedding blunders, and it's also a waste of your money.

Call to confirm the delivery and order of your cake once or twice during the planning months, then once again several days before the wedding.

Why pay over a hundred dollars for a cake when you can borrow tier pans, buy cake mixes and frosting, and make your own wedding cake? Just get a how-to book from the library and create your own wedding cake. It's really not that difficult. If you don't trust yourself, take a cake-decorating course at a nearby school. You'll still spend much less than you would have spent on a bakery cake.

Bakery wedding cake	$85–$200
Homemade cake	$20–$40

Making it from scratch is even less expensive—especially if you buy all your supplies in bulk or from a discount supplier. Prices here could go as low as ten dollars, depending on the size.

Have a relative or friend make the wedding cake for you as a gift.

Make sure you choose fillings and frosting that will do well in the weather. A hot summer day could cause your cake to melt right off the table. It has happened. A butter-cream frosting usually holds up better than a plain whipped cream frosting. Keep the cake in the shade and as cool as possible on warm days.

Look through advertisements for a person who makes and decorates wedding cakes as a side job. Ads for this service can be found in regular classified ads or the bridal section of your town newspaper. Investigate and compare prices carefully.

Consider hiring a high school home economics class to do your wedding cake. The teacher will appreciate your offering the experience to the class, and you'll get a good cake for a low price.

Make the groom's cake yourself.

Have a relative or friend make the groom's cake.

Skip the groom's cake altogether, especially if you're having a small or informal wedding.

On Top of the Cake

You could buy one of those traditional cake-top decorations at the bakery, or you could put something else on the cake:

Top off your cake with a special item or gift. A jeweled ostrich egg is a gorgeous topper, but just make sure the baker knows exactly how much it weighs and its size so the precious thing doesn't fall off the cake onto the floor. The same goes for anything else you're planning to top your cake with.

Top your cake with items of your heritage, such as tiny national flags or dolls in traditional dress. You may already own these things, so it will be a personal touch as well.

Decorate your cake with flowers you've picked yourself. Just wash them well, let them air dry, and make sure they're not poisonous. Check with your baker as to which flowers usually go on cakes as decorations, then check with your florist about the safety of those flowers. Saving money should never be a health hazard.

Or see if you can negotiate the cake top for free as part of the cake package.

The Cake Cutter

Don't choose from those offered in bridal salons or bridal catalogs. They're very often not the best buy.

Buy a simple silver cake cutter set and decorate the handle with ribbons or silk flowers.

Have a young sibling or a special friend give the cake cutter to you as a wedding gift. You may even receive a pretty engraved one.

If you're not one to treasure your wedding cake cutter forever, just use the reception hall's serving knife.

See if your bakery offers a wedding cake cutter set as part of the wedding cake package.

33

Favors and Mementos

Favors

Wine bottles with personalized labels stating the names of the bride and groom and the wedding date are a popular choice among brides today, but that's unfortunately an expensive idea. If you must go this route, comparison shop by calling different wineries and asking about their personalized favor services. Good researching here can save you fifty to a hundred dollars.

Check with liquor wholesalers to see if you can get little bottles of wine or Kahlua in bulk. They may not have the fancy labels with your name on them, but they're just as nice. Some brides have even been able to get a peach wine to match their wedding color scheme.

The usual sugar-coated almonds wrapped in tulle and ribbons can turn into a costly venture. Shop around for the almonds in different markets—not bridal specialty stores—and look for sales on tulle and ribbon.

Homemade chocolate candies packaged in little gift boxes are an economical choice, and you can attach to them the symbolism of the sweetness of marriage. It's not uncommon for brides to make these favors for under twenty-five dollars for all the boxes they'll need.

Instead of store-bought sachets, create your own. Just buy potpourri at a discount store in bulk—or make your own following directions in a craft book—and sew it into little packages or wrap them into bundles with squares of tulle. You can always ask a talented friend to help with this job.

Start planting seeds now so that you can give out as favors tiny seedlings that your guest can plant in your honor. Ask your florist for the best varieties. One bride used seeds she'd gathered last season from her own flowering plants. At no cost to her, she grew one hundred and fifty seedlings as her favors.

An inexpensive wedding favor, and one with much sentimental value, is a personal message printed on parchment (by computer or by hand) then rolled into a scroll and sealed with a gold sticker or a wax print. Another variation on this idea is a poem or quote suitable for framing.

Other Favor Sources to Try

Celebrations in Green by Expressions (seedlings)	716-266-6519
Chocolate Photos	800-526-3437

34

Wedding Night Accommodations

After the reception, you and your new husband may be whisked right off to the airport to catch the plane headed for your honeymoon spot or you may find yourself with a night to spend alone before catching that plane in the morning. Many brides and grooms choose to spend their first night together as husband and wife in the honeymoon suite of a nearby luxury hotel, often adding midnight room service to their bill. Unfortunately, while this is considered by many the way to go, it's also costly.

Get a plain old regular room instead. Do you really need to pay three times as much for pink walls, nice artwork, a scenic view, and a heart-shaped bed? You'll probably be somewhat tired after the excitement of the day, and all the facilities and extras may be lost on you. Besides, it's the first night of your honeymoon. You won't be looking at the view or admiring the artwork anyway.

See if you can get your first night's room for free as part of the group discount in the hotel in which your visiting family and friends are staying. One bride negotiated a free weekend stay in the hotel: savings of two hundred and fifty dollars. Just don't tell your guests which room you're in, or they may find it funny to call you or surprise you.

If you have your own place, why not spend the first night there? After all, it's free, and your first night together can make those familiar surroundings new and exciting.

Perhaps friends or relatives can let you use their guest cottage. It can be their wedding gift to you.

If you'll have to catch a flight at a faraway airport early the next morning, you may choose to spend the night at a hotel near there. Airport-access hotels are often over-priced due to demand, so you'll definitely want to get a no-frills room there. The honeymoon suite will defi-nitely be too costly.

However, if you just won't have it any other way—if you *must* have the honeymoon suite—comparison shop around town. You can at least find the lowest price available.

The first night spent in a luxury hotel is a great gift idea for parents to consider. They may have wanted to pay for your honeymoon, but they'll be happy you've found them this equally special gesture at less of a blow to their own savings. Discuss this idea with them, or with any other relative or friend who might find this an appropri-ate gift—perhaps the people who introduced you.

35

Planning the Honeymoon

The grand total of this trip alone could equal the price tag for the entire wedding, so you'll want to spend your money wisely. The honeymoon is another one of those big ticket items it's best not to scrimp on. Trying too hard to save money may result in a disappointing vacation in the long run. The key to cutting honeymoon costs without failing your expectations and dreams lies in smart shopping and lots of research. Don't let the travel industry target you as a less than savvy traveler with lots of gift money to spend.

Where to Begin

Before you start flipping through the travel section of the newspaper or those vacation reviews in the bridal magazines, set your honeymoon budget. A good rule of thumb is to plan on spending a set amount of money you already have available. Don't plan a three-thousand-dollar vacation hoping you'll get at least that much in wedding gift money to cover the cost. If you've estimated wrong, you'll begin married life in debt. So plan on a medium budget (not *too* inexpensive or you'll feel like you've ripped yourself off).

Start by searching through travel magazines and brochures to get an idea of where you both would like to spend your honeymoon. Make a wish list that will allow you to compare the pros and cons of each destination.

Make a list of what you *don't* want. You may not want a ski vacation or one of those island trips where there's nothing to do all day but lie on the beach. You may be supersensitive to the sun and therefore unwilling to go to the tropics, or you may not want to travel overseas. Before you start your search for your honeymoon spot, it's important that you have some guidelines. The thousands of ideas you come across will be that much easier to narrow down.

Check with friends or relatives who travel often or who have just returned from their own honeymoon. Where did they go? Would they recommend the same place?

Don't fall for travel scams. If you receive a postcard claiming that you've won a cruise, but all you have to do is send $10 and your credit card number for verification of your identity, don't do it. You haven't won anything. It's a trick, and the authorities are cracking down on the scam artists who are perpetuating this kind of fraud. So don't believe postcards or mass mailings that sound too good to be true. They are. Now, if Ed McMahon shows up on your doorstep, you're all set. (Just make sure it *is* Ed McMahon.)

The Travel Agent

Do use a travel agent. The service is free in most cases, and you're more likely to find out about specials and less expensive packages through a professional who is paid to know these things.

Use your regular travel agent, the one you've booked trips through for years. You can be sure of his or her reliability.

Ask friends and relatives if they'd recommend their travel agent for the job. Again, you'll have evidence of that person's reliability and timeliness.

When looking for your own travel agent, consider whether you want the personal service of a smaller agency or the wide-range exposure and knowledge of a larger agency. Both have their pros and cons, so weigh them carefully before you choose.

Make sure the travel agent you choose is a member of the American Society of Travel Agents. Ask for credentials, or check to see the agent's affiliation listed on his or her business card. Check with the Better Business Bureau to see if any charges or complaints have been directed against your agent or the agency.

Does your travel agent seem interested in your wishes, or is he or she just typing codes into the computer with an I-can't-wait-for-lunch attitude? Does she seem knowledgeable? Does she know where to find out such things as a particular destination's climate, code of dress, and customs rules? Does she speak of her own travels? Often, your personal feelings about the travel agent can give you a clue as to whether or not you should be trusting her with these important arrangements.

Go through your company's travel agent. You may get a break if the service is available to you.

You could do all the work yourself, using toll-free numbers to request information, calling airlines directly, and using your home computer to reserve your tickets. However, this does take up a lot of your time, and some of these ways to gather prices and times could cost you money. Some major airlines' numbers are listed at the end of this chapter. If you already subscribe to a service such as Prodigy, which lets you check prices not only on American Airlines flights but on other carriers' as well, you're better able to collect your information and reserve flights yourself.

Choosing a Destination

Write to tourist offices for lists of hotels, events, and facilities. Your research could turn up one of those hidden gems most tourists miss. One bride used this information to find special rates, off-times, and incredible sales and saved one hundred fifty dollars.

Check your library's travel books. Volumes of low-cost traveling guides have been published, and they're free for the asking. Titles such as *Bermuda on Ten Dollars a Day* can save you a bundle and tip you off to many free attractions.

Consider the time of year—Part One: The Off-Season. Plan your honeymoon for a place that will be in its off-season. Rates will be lower, special packages will become available, and you'll find fewer crowds and greater bargains everywhere. You can find out about each of your potential destinations' off-season months either in their board of tourism's brochures or through your travel agent.

Consider the time of year—Part Two: The Weather. Speaking of the season, look at the usual weather patterns of the region you'll be visiting during your honeymoon. Is it going to be hurricane season then? Tornado time? Bad weather can take time away from your vacation, either by keeping you indoors during eight straight days of gale-force winds and rain or by making you miss a few days of your vacation because inclement weather has canceled or delayed your flight there. Again, check in travel brochures or with your agent.

Pay attention to travel advertisements. Price wars and seasonal specials can reveal great discounts. Just pay attention to the fine print before you call that toll-free number.

Look at the international political scene. Is your dream destination currently undergoing some civil unrest that could erupt into full-scale battling? Time spent with five hundred people in a bomb shelter and bullets whistling overhead can put a serious damper on your trip. Check ahead of time by asking your travel agent and by checking international travel magazines that have a danger zone column.

Try a nonhoneymoon destination. Hotels and resorts specifically geared toward honeymooners are often much higher priced than nonspecialized alternatives. You may be the only honeymooners in the pool, but you won't notice.

Don't travel so far away. The farther you go, the more you'll pay. Visit someplace closer to home . . . like a nearby island or a resort town in your own state.

We enjoyed our trip upstate every bit as much as if we'd gone to another country. Neither of us had ever been skiing, so it was a wonderful adventure. Plus we saved three hundred dollars in airfare.

—Darlene, bride.

Foreign travel is, of course, much more expensive than a domestic getaway. Distance airfare aside, you're going to have to deal with higher prices in a tourist city and the fluctuating value of the American dollar in foreign currency.

Is there another U.S. state or Canadian province you've always thought about visiting? Your honeymoon might be the perfect money-saving opportunity. For free information—including some gorgeous books and pamphlets—try some of the following toll-free numbers (a lot of cities and states have them these days):

Alabama Bureau of Tourism & Travel	800-252-2262
Bahama Tourist Office	800-228-5173
Bermuda Department of Tourism	800-223-6107

Connecticut State Tourist Information	800-282-6863
Delaware Tourism Office	800-441-8846
Jersey/Cape May County	800-227-2297
Kentucky Department of Travel	800-225-8747
Key West Chamber of Commerce	800-648-6269
Michigan Travel Bureau	800-543-2937
Minnesota Office of Tourism	800-345-2537
Mississippi Division of Tourism	800-647-2290
Montana Travel Promotion Office	800-541-1447
Nebraska State Tourism	800-228-4307
Nevada Tourism Commission	800-638-2328
New Hampshire Vacations	800-542-2331
Niagara Falls & Niagara County Tourist Information	800-338-7890
North Carolina Travel & Tourism	800-847-4862
Northern Kentucky Visitors Bureau	800-447-8489
Oklahoma State Tourism & Recreational Dept.	800-654-8240
Oregon City Chamber of Commerce	800-424-3002
Puerto Rico Tourism Company	800-223-6530

Quebec Tourism	800-363-7777
South Carolina Tourism Division	800-872-3505
State of Baja California	800-225-2786
State of Louisiana Office of Tourism	800-227-4386
Tourist Information of Las Vegas Club Guide	800-426-8695
Utah County Travel Council & Visitor Bureau	800-222-8824
Virginia Division of Tourism	800-248-4833

For more information, and for additional money-saving resources, check your library for the AT&T TOLL FREE 800 DIRECTORY. In it, you'll find the phone numbers of such valuable offices as tourist groups, tourist attractions, discounters of all kinds—and the calls are free from almost anywhere in the country.

Are Those Honeymoon Packages Worth It?

A hotel's honeymooner's paradise package may turn out to be less of a bargain than it seems. After all, will you really need everything included in the package? Will you want to eat three meals a day in your hotel's restaurant? Will you be playing golf every day? Scuba diving three times in a week? And will you really want to spend your time on a double-decker bus tour with stops at working farms? Take a good look at each element of the package, circle the ones you're sure you'll need, then price only those items separately. You may have to play mathematician, but you could end up with a better price if you're footing the bill just for your room and only the meals and extras you know you'll enjoy.

When considering packages, remember to add in the following to the prices: airport arrival and departure taxes, room tax, electricity tax (if applicable), baggage charges, facility fees, cover charges to the nightclub and local attractions, gratuities, service charges for your traveler's checks, transportation rental, and the food and drinks you'll have outside of the meals included in your package.

Comparison shop between separate resorts' packages, remembering to look for all the hidden taxes and fees in the small print.

Investigate the cancellation details. Is any deposit non-refundable?

Booking Your Room

You will certainly spend a good amount of money here. In fact, you may have been saving money throughout the planning of the wedding just so you and your husband can have top-of-the-line honeymoon accommodations. But you'd still do well to get the best buys you can for your money. This includes protecting your investment with good record keeping and organization.

The big, fancy hotels with the names known around the world are certainly going to be more expensive than somewhat less flashy ones. Try a three-star hotel instead of a four-star one. You'll hardly notice the difference.

When investigating the larger, more luxurious hotels in the big cities, see if their weekend rates are better than their weekday rates. Most big hotels that cater to week-day business clients will offer Friday through Sunday discounts, and these are well worth looking into.

Do you really need the Honeymoon Suite? Usually, the biggest, most luxurious rooms with the fireplaces and the personal swimming pools go for top dollar, so consider the savings of a smaller deluxe room with the necessities: a bed and a bathroom. Even the view is negotiable. Of course, this is not to say you should book the dumpiest room they have. You'd be setting yourself up for a huge disappointment when the room doesn't match your fantasies of the perfect honeymoon. Just trim the gaudy extras away. You'll still be in romantic surroundings.

The Honeymoon Flight

Check all the major airlines and comparison shop. (See the resource lists at the end of this chapter.)

Check the price differences between flying on a weekend and flying on a weekday. A ticket for three hundred dollars less might make it worth your while to take a Monday flight.

Fly at an off-peak hour. For instance, a discounted midnight flight would be perfect for you if you'd like to get a head start on your honeymoon right from your reception. One bride saved eighty dollars on plane tickets with this option.

Keep restrictions in mind when inquiring about low fares. A particular bargain may require you to stay overnight on a Sunday or pay a nonrefundable fee six months before your honeymoon. If you can meet the requirements, no problem. If not, you could be facing a wasted sum of money.

Another factor controlling airline prices is the season in which you'll be flying, so keep ticket costs in mind when choosing the date of your wedding and honeymoon. A Christmas weekend wedding may seem like a wonderful idea at first, but it won't be as grand when you're paying three times the normal cost of a ticket and facing holiday rush crowds. Other holiday seasons to look out for: Thanksgiving, New Year's, Easter, spring break, and basically most of the summer. Just do your best to avoid high travel times if you can.

See if you'd be better off with a nonstop flight. Direct flights make stops at certain cities along the way to your destination, and the delays could take up your valuable time, especially if you're on a shorter honeymoon. Ask your travel agent if nonstop flights are more or less expensive than other types of flights available to you.

On the other hand, some honeymooners see those flights with six-hour layovers to be more of a bargain than a pain in the neck. After all, if your discounted flight has a long break in between a change of planes, you've just gotten yourself to a distant major city that you may have enough time to explore a little for just the price of a taxi. Just make sure you allow yourself enough time to check in for your next flight, and be back at the airport in time to catch that flight. Margie and Matt, recent newlyweds, spent their layover time in Boston checking out historical landmarks and sharing a cup of clam chowder by the waterfront.

You may think that you're getting the best deal possible when you ask for economy tickets, but there may be better deals elsewhere. This is where your travel agent is invaluable. Always ask for the lowest fare available instead of assuming the so-called economy tickets are the best buy.

First-class tickets can cost several times the price of business or coach. What for? Some more leg room? An eight-course meal? Save the difference in expense— you're getting to your destination at the same time as those folks up in the leather seats.

Traveling standby may seem like a bargain, but it can be more trouble than it's worth. Do you really want to start off your honeymoon waiting for twelve hours in an airport for a cancellation so there's room for you on board?

Look into charter flights. Some companies are listed in the resources at the end of this chapter. Special arrangements can turn up big savings for you. See what your travel agent knows about these flights.

Don't go for ultraspecials without checking them out thoroughly first. Read all the fine print, get your travel agent's advice, then proceed only with a money-back guarantee.

Check cancellation guarantees on all flights you consider. A reputable airline will allow you at least a partial refund in case of emergency or mishap. You may want to consider cancellation insurance. It may cost you a few bucks extra, but your returns in case of a change in plans will reward you.

Get a written copy of your itinerary, including all flight numbers and airline confirmation numbers. On this record of your reservation, record your travel agent's name and the date and time you made your travel arrangements . . . just for your own assurance.

Get yourself the best bargain possible. See if your student or military ID can net you a traveler discount.

If you have a friend or relative employed by the airline or travel industry, see if you can swing a ride on their discount. Make it their wedding gift to you.

Ask your travel agent about their connections with a travel consolidator. The travel consolidator is sold discount tickets from an airline that hasn't been able to fill a plane. The consolidator then arranges to sell those discounted tickets through your travel agent at a cut rate for you. This may mean discounts of 25 percent, 30 percent, or more, and such savings may make you forget about the usual accompanying travel restrictions such as no advance seat selection, no frequent flyer mileage, and having to fly at an off-hour. See the resource section at the end of this chapter.

Use your own frequent flier miles to get an upgrade or even free tickets. If you have a year or two of planning time before the wedding, get on a frequent flier plan if you'll be doing much flying. One new bride racked up so much mileage visiting her fiancé in California, her air miles credits earned her one free plane ticket for her honeymoon. That was a three-hundred-dollar savings.

Ask your travel agent about promotional fares. They too may have some travel restrictions, such as time of flight and no frequent flyer miles, but they could get you to your honeymoon for a reasonable price.

Ask your travel agent also about fare assurance programs. That way, if a better price comes along for the tickets you purchased at the previous rate, you could be given the tickets for the lower fare.

Confirm your flight twenty-four to forty-eight hours in advance. Foreign travel confirmations should be made two to three days in advance.

When you're checking in at the airport, see if you can arrange an upgrade. With some airlines, you can get your seating assignment changed for only thirty or forty dollars. Just be sure to arrive at the airport early, and be prepared to have your request put on standby. This means you'll find out if you've gotten the upgrade at about the same time you're getting on the plane.

Trains and Other Transportation

Compare train travel prices with airline fares. You might find a bargain in a special, and you'll get the wonderful view of a scenic cross-country ride. See the resource section at the end of this chapter.

Look for train travel specials in advertisements.

Special train and bus passes can offer you unlimited travel. If you're both adventurers and wouldn't mind a honeymoon-on-the-go, you'll have a pass for an active and scenic honeymoon plus no huge hotel fees—just the two of you together on the road.

If your honeymoon location is close, drive your own car. Just make sure it's in working order first, and plan out the most direct and economical route. Again, this is a scenic and adventurous choice. One bride, Mandy, used her local AAA's services and had them map out the best route for her and her husband's drive to Colorado. They saved one hundred dollars in gas and lodging with this new plan.

Cruises

Visit your travel agent to collect as much literature as you can on the different cruise lines. Keep in mind the kind of cruise you'd like. An active one? A relaxing one? One with many stops at different islands for sightseeing and souvenir shopping? If you have the kind of cruise you'd like in mind, you'll have a much easier time matching your preferences up with the available cruise tours. Use the resource section at the end of this chapter for toll-free numbers and contacts.

Ask your family and friends who cruise often if they'd like to recommend their favorite ships and tours.

The location of your cabin can affect the price of your tickets. Top deck, outside, and center of the boat cabins are more expensive than their opposites, and most cruise goers claim that a room right on the waterline provides a much more stable ride. Look at the positioning of the rooms on those color-coded boat charts you'll find in most cruise brochures, and pay special attention to the square footage of the rooms you're considering.

Out-of-the-Ordinary Honeymoon Destinations

For all of the romance and quiet seclusion and none of the honeymoon industry's expensive extras, try a getaway at a bed and breakfast. Check your library for a free guidebook of the best.

If you're comfortable with the idea or have done it before, a home exchange is a good way to stay in a different city for free. All you have to do is let the owner of that home stay at your place for free, although much care must be taken to set good ground rules before you leave.

Camping is a romantic way to spend your honeymoon . . . alone together in the middle of nature with the moon and the stars above. It may not be a week at a four-star hotel, but it's still a great vacation for less of a dent in your budget. A hint: Make sure you're not planning this camping trip during your region's rainy season. Getting stuck in your tent all week may sound romantic, but you still have to take into account the cold, the mud, the after-rain mosquitoes. . . . For information on camping locations and regulations, write to:

National Park Service
U.S. Dept. of the Interior
18th & C Streets NW
Washington, DC 20240

Try a canoeing or sailing adventure honeymoon. You just set out with your own or borrowed equipment with a map and plenty of instruction, and you're set for a wild and memorable ride.

Try the ocean, lakes, mountains, and cities near you. Some of the best-kept secrets are hidden closer to home than you think.

Your Honeymoon Preparations

Apply for your passport way in advance. Don't leave the job for the last minute—passports take several weeks, if not months, to process. Don't be one of those unorganized brides who don't get their passports in time for their European honeymoon and then have to cancel the trip with no refund. How painful.

Prepare your luggage for the trip by making sure your luggage tags have your correct name and address on them. Pack a sheet of paper stating your name and honeymoon destination inside your suitcases just in case they get misdirected.

Don't overpack. A too-heavy case could wind up costing you extra. Most airlines have weight restrictions, and their extra fees aren't minor.

Try to pack everything you'll need on your honeymoon. Having to buy lotion or toothpaste at your hotel's gift shop could cost you a lot of money. Items stocked there are overpriced, particularly film for your camera. So pack well.

Pack in your carry-on bag the following items:

Your tickets
Your passports
A copy of your
    marriage license
Traveler's checks
Credit cards
Itinerary with contact
    phone numbers
Hotel confirmation
    information
Car rental
    confirmation
    information

Your hotel's name and
    address
Your eyeglasses or
    contact lenses
Lens-cleaning solution
Contraception
Prescription
    medications
Camera and film
Addresses for postcards
Extra clothes in case
    of a layover
Your good jewelry

Set up a house sitter to watch your home and possessions and feed your pets while you're away. Give the house sitter a list of important phone numbers and instructions (such as trash day and directions to local stores), and leave explicit rules about parties, guests, and access to your food. A non-live-in could simply take in your mail and newspapers, feed and walk the dog, and park the car in your driveway to give the appearance that someone is at home. When the visiting caretaker is away, continue the illusion with timed lights and a timed stereo. Automatic sensor lights that come on when motion is detected by the doors or windows are another break-in deterrent.

Save Money on Your Honeymoon

Eat some casual meals during your honeymoon. If you take every meal in the hotel's dress-up dining room, you'll pay much more than if you had grabbed a sandwich and fries at the pool bar for lunch a few times. Besides, you won't have to miss a moment in the sun to go in, shower, and dress for a meal.

Don't drink alcohol. At least not at every meal and at every trip to the poolside bar. As you know, alcoholic drinks are much more expensive than the nonalcoholic kinds—especially when you add on the resort's already higher price tags. A frozen daiquiri at a Caribbean bar last summer cost one bride eleven dollars. And it was served in a plastic cup! Be prepared for high prices at the beverage and food concessions.

Room service means an extra charge just for the waiter to walk up to your room. Why not carry a bottle of champagne and a fruit platter upstairs yourself, or sneak down and pick up something to surprise your husband while he's running a bubble bath for you?

Get a room with a refrigerator and a stove unit so that you can prepare some simpler snacks and drinks. Go to a nearby market in town and stock up on sodas and fruit and keep those in your refrigerator.

Stay clear of those little stocked refrigerators that seem to offer you every kind of drink and snack under the sun. You will be overcharged for each of those items.

Your membership in a professional organization could lead to discounts for you if you ask for them. Talk to your organization's headquarters.

If you're in a foreign country, don't exchange your money at the street vendor's stand, in airports and train stations, or at tourist attractions. You'll get better rates and therefore more for your dollar if you change your money at reputable banks.

Pay careful attention to the customs regulations of the area. Make sure your souvenirs can be legally brought home and that you haven't purchased more than you can take home duty-free. You will have to pay customs on anything over a certain price limit.

Be careful about using your credit card when you're buying items or services overseas. You may wind up paying the dollar rate at the time of billing rather than at the time of purchase. If the dollar has fallen into a slump since then, you're actually getting that great buy for much less of a bargain. Then again, your credit card company *can* offer you some security in your purchases by investigating trouble and possibly reimbursing you for lost or stolen merchandise.

Use traveler's checks that can be used at face value and don't charge a service fee.

Use your auto club's regular discounts.

Don't rent a car at the airport. Rental agencies there may be overpriced. See the list of car rental agencies in the resource section at the end of this chapter.

Rent a smaller car without a radio, power windows, and all the fancy extras.

Is it less expensive to rent a car for a week than for four days? Look into the agency's pricing and do some creative figuring.

Reserve your car ahead of time so you're not left renting a van at extra cost because it's all they have.

Keep track of the car's mileage. You'll want to make sure you're charged the correct amount. Just being on your honeymoon won't protect you from getting ripped off. You'll have to protect yourselves.

Plan all your car travel for one or two days so that you're getting the most for a smaller rental time. It doesn't make sense to rent the car for a week and only use it two or three days.

Rent bikes or scooters instead. Comparison shop around your honeymoon spot for the best rates, or ask the hotel's social guide to help you track down the best prices.

Get bus and train passes so you won't have to take expensive taxis around town. There's no better way to absorb the local flavor. One married couple figured their train transport saved them sixty-five dollars in taxi fares.

Many big-city theaters sell same-day performance tickets at discounted prices. If you're a smart shopper, you could wind up with prime seats at lower than low prices.

Look for free tours and attractions in your guidebooks. They will have every bit as much local flavor as those that charge for admittance.

Buy small, inexpensive souvenirs. Remember the luggage weight requirements? You'll have to meet those on the way home, too. Or take home free souvenirs: coasters, bar napkins, brochures, shells, rocks, even some sand or ocean water in a small bottle.

Resources

Resources for Airline Research

Air Canada	800-776-3000
America West	800-247-5692
American Airlines	800-433-7300
British Airways	800-247-9297
Continental Airlines	800-525-0280
Delta Airlines	800-221-1212
KLM Royal Dutch Airlines	800-374-7747
Kiwi International Airlines	800-538-5494
Northwest Airlines	800-225-2525
TWA	800-221-2000
USAir	800-428-4322
United Airlines	800-241-6522
Virgin Atlantic Airways	800-862-8621

Resource for Train Travel Research

Amtrak	800-872-7245
Eurailpass	P.O. Box 10383
	Stamford, CT 06904

Resources for Cruise Research

Carnival Cruise Lines	see your travel agent
Dolphin Cruise Lines	see your travel agent
Majesty Cruises	see your travel agent
Norwegian Cruise Line	800-262-4NCL
Princess Cruises	see your travel agent
Royal Caribbean	800-727-2717

Resources for Hotel Chain Research

Best Western	800-528-1234
Embassy Suites	800-362-2779
Holiday Inn	check your Yellow Pages
Howard Johnsons	check your Yellow Pages
Marriott	800-228-9290
Ramada	800-228-2828
Quality, Comfort, Clarion Inns	check your Yellow Pages

Resources for Rental Car Companies

Alamo	800-327-9633
Automate	800-633-2824
Dollar	800-800-4000
Hertz	800-654-3131

Check your Yellow Pages for other companies near you.

Note: *Be sure to check with the rental companies you call about their restrictions and age requirements. Some companies will not rent cars or other vehicles to persons under 25 years of age. Find this out before you reserve your car.*

Resources for International Charter Lines

LTU International Airways	800-888-0200
(from selected cities to Germany)	
Condor	800-782-2424
(from selected cities to Frankfurt)	

Resources for Travel Clubs

Travel clubs offer discounts on plane tickets, hotel reservations, and other attractions, but they do require a membership fee; most run anywhere from $25 to $50. So this type of plan may work well for you if you travel often, or plan to travel often in the near future. Call these numbers for more information:

Concierge	800-346-1022
CUC Travel Services Inc.	800-248-4234
Encore	800-638-0930
Traveler's Plus/World Unlimited	800-237-0952

Resources for Vacation Organizations

Condolink	800-733-4445
Hideaways International	800-843-4433

Include these numbers in your vacation research, and ask plenty of questions. It's also a good idea to ask for references, so you can speak to other travelers who have used these services.

36

Your Trousseau

You don't have to buy a whole new wardrobe. That may have been the case in the old days, but now it's smarter to just buy a few special new pieces and fill in the gaps with your own favorite vacation clothes and shoes.

Buy clothing you can use again. One-time wearings aren't worth the ticket price.

Stay away from top-name, high-priced clothing stores. Why get one item for two hundred dollars when you can get five great new things for the same price elsewhere?

Don't shop in bridal boutiques for your honeymoon outfits and lingerie. Go to regular department stores and mid-priced lingerie boutiques instead for better choices and better prices.

Shop at discount stores and in outlets for incredible bargains in your areas. Some moderately priced clothing chains: Dress Barn, Hit or Miss, Marshalls, Mandees, T. J. Maxx.

Look through catalogs, keeping an eye out for sales and making sure to add in shipping costs before you decide on an item. A few good catalog companies to consider:

Newport News	800-688-2830
JCPenney	800-222-6161
JRT	800-285-4100

Don't overbuy, using your honeymoon as an excuse to splurge on yourself. Of course the temptation will be there, but act in moderation. Consider the money you save to be money in your airfare fund.

If you have shoes that are in good condition and are suitable for your vacation, use them. Besides the money you save, you're also saving the pain and trouble of breaking in new shoes on a tour. There's no time for blisters on a honeymoon.

Don't shop for your trousseau until after your bridal showers. You just may get all the lingerie and robes you'll ever need as gifts. One bride originally budgeted two hundred dollars for her honeymoon lingerie. After receiving a roomful of teddies and bustiers, she redirected that money to her attendants' gifts. Overall, she saved two hundred dollars.

A final note: Pamper yourself with new lingerie and undergarments more than with outer clothing. A trousseau fund spent entirely on teddies and garters will make for a more interesting trip than new shorts and earrings.

Your Going-Away Outfit

Instead of buying a brand-new, expensive dress specifically for the trip from the reception to the airport (or from the reception to the hotel), use one of your honeymoon dresses.

Perhaps your going-away dress can be a gift from your mother or grandmother.

Or just make your grand exit from the reception in your wedding gown, then change at home into casual clothes for more comfortable traveling to the airport or hotel. You won't even need a going-away outfit.

37

Guest Lodging

Luckily, modern standards are leaning toward releasing your family from paying for all the visiting friends' and family's lodging before the wedding. Yet even though the checks are not being written in your hand, you can still find savings for those people who have come to share your day.

Comparison shop for the best-priced hotels in town, taking care not to book a dive just because of its low prices. A room in a cockroach-infested truck stop is no way to welcome your favorite people. So look around, ask to see the rooms, and talk to people who are actually staying at the hotel. See the hotel resources list in Chapter 35.

A good idea is to book the rooms in the hotel where the reception is being held. That way, no one has to get in a car and drive after the party. You may even get a special discount.

Ask about group rates. If you're planning to book a certain number of rooms, you'll undoubtedly get a break. Jo, a bride, estimated her savings at twenty-five dollars per room.

Plan for your guests to share their rooms. Two young couples can share the room with the two double beds, and the family of five can arrange themselves in the same kind of room instead of using one for Mom and Dad and one for the kids. Besides being a savings to you, it actually is more fun for them. No doubt they'll all have their doors open and be wandering around the halls as if the building were a college dorm.

Don't let these guests come into town too early. Two days ahead of time is more than enough. You don't want to have to entertain them while there's so much for you to do, and unnecessary days' accommodations just rack up extra hotel bills. So make it clear that everyone is to arrive only a day or two before the wedding.

If there aren't too many people coming in from way out of town, consider putting them all up at your place, at relatives' homes, and at kind neighbors' houses. Again, besides the obvious savings, it's a fun change of pace to be able to spend time with a houseguest.

Place inexpensive gifts in your guests' rooms. Good ideas are baskets of soft drinks and snacks, maps and listings of interesting things to see and do in the area, and toys and games for the kids. Always include a personal note, thanking your guests for coming to town.

38

The Bridal Luncheons

An informal brunch or luncheon is always a good alternative to the fancier, more expensive bridal soirees. Instead of having it at a restaurant, hold the luncheon at your home. Most brides who opt for this kind of get-together can expect to save up to one hundred dollars, depending on the number of guests and the menu.

If you'll be hosting the party at home, prepare light foods, appetizers, or an inexpensive entree that can feed a group. Or just have dessert.

If you've decided it would be best to meet at a café, do so with a dutch treat arrangement.

Or you could skip the whole luncheon idea and opt instead for a shower or rehearsal dinner to take its place.

39

The Rehearsal Dinner

Whether or not the groom's family is planning on financing the rehearsal dinner, you can still save money for whoever is picking up the bill. There's no need to have a formal, catered rehearsal dinner. While some brides may have the funds for a professional photographer, a seven-course meal, and strolling violinists, the rest of us find it much simpler—and more enjoyable—to have a more informal dinner. After all, the important dress-up affair with the pricey meal comes tomorrow. Who needs top-of-the-line two days in a row?

You'll do better to plan a more casual evening. It will give you all much-needed time to relax and enjoy one another's company, and no one has to wear stockings or a tie.

Your informal rehearsal dinner could be a pizza party, a barbecue in the yard, a pool party, or even a trip to the beach.

You can still have the sit-down dinner. Just serve it at home instead of at a fancy restaurant. Choose from inexpensive meals that stretch to feed a crowd: pasta, stew, Mexican fare, homemade pizzas set up in a make-your-own arrangement.

If you've all agreed to go out to a favorite restaurant, arrange for everyone to split the bill, or . . .

Just have dessert and coffee at a nice café. The term *rehearsal dinner* doesn't *have* to mean dinner.

Skip the professional photographer. While you'll undoubtedly want some record of this gathering, it's enough to take your own shots or get copies of those taken by your family and friends. There's no need to spend five hundred dollars for a professional photo session tonight.

40

Your Personal Beauty Care

Of course you'll want to look your absolute best for your wedding, and a little bit of the royal treatment is not out of line for the bride. But don't go overboard. I'm not going to suggest that you spend absolutely no money on primping. Just don't spend hundreds of dollars on brand-name cosmetics, and don't go to an overpriced salon just for the glamorous experience. You can pamper yourself for less. You should avoid certain treatments anyway right before your wedding, in case of a beauty mishap.

Don't buy all new makeup just for your wedding. You're better off using your own makeup for the more natural look you're used to. Some less frugal brides have reported dropping one hundred twenty-five dollars on glamour-line cosmetics. The rest of us could find a better use for that money.

If you must buy new makeup, don't go for the disgustingly overpriced kinds. Comparison shop for bargains, or see if you can find the same brand and color you normally use.

Scout out the makeup counters for free samples. Just one of those little tubes of lipstick is enough to keep you in the pink throughout your wedding day. Just don't attempt to grab fourteen of those little samples. There's a difference between making good use of a sample and taking advantage.

Get samples for each bridesmaid to use. They can grab their own when they're out shopping with you, and they've saved ten to twenty dollars as well.

All of your bridesmaids and honor attendants can use the same bottle of nail polish. No need for each to buy her own.

Do your own makeup. After all, you'll do the most natural-looking job on yourself. A professional might overpaint you . . . and then expect to be paid for the stuff you'll just wipe off later anyway. Besides, some brides find it relaxing to do their own makeup on their wedding day. Just give yourself plenty of time.

Professional makeup application	$25–$40
Do it yourself	free

Don't attempt to give yourself a home perm if you've never had one before. This is no time to take chances with your hair just to save a few bucks. Instead, go to your trusted beautician. Your hair is worth the money.

If you've always dyed your hair and you're comfortable with the way it turns out every time, then there's no reason you shouldn't do your own touch-ups rather than go to a salon.

Salon dye job	$20–$50
At-home dye job	$5–$15

Few brides would take the chance of cutting their own hair just for the money saved. A good haircut is the basis of the bride's style, and it's also an inexpensive way to get that pampered feeling without the full line of extravagances. So the best way to watch your finances when it comes to haircuts is simply to stay with your regular stylist. A too-cheap salon you've found on a back road may give terrible, disastrous haircuts, and a gaudy, overpriced one will give you a standard chop with an outrageous bill attached. The best way to save money on your haircut: just have a wash and cut, instead of the wash, cut, and style. You won't be getting your hair cut on your wedding day anyway, so you don't really need the costly styling.

Have a bridesmaid or even a neighbor French braid your hair for you if you like the look but can't do it right yourself. The favor saves you salon prices, which can run up to thirty dollars for this simple service.

Have a bridesmaid pin your headpiece on for you. Why would you need to go to a salon for that, and then have to drive home with your headpiece on?

Set your own hair with steam rollers. Practice for the right look several days in advance.

Use your own home waxing kit rather than go to a salon. Again, savings can reach anywhere from fifteen to thirty dollars.

Use your own home bleaching kit instead of going to a salon. Just be sure to follow the directions carefully— you don't want burn marks on your upper lip.

Electrolysis is one of those things you might be better off going to a professional for, unless, of course, you have your own home kit and have been using it for a while. Then it's OK to save the salon fee with a do-it-yourself job.

Salon fee for electrolysis	$30
Home job	free

Worship the sun instead of a tanning booth. Just be smart about sunblock and avoid direct sun/UV times— 11 A.M.–3 P.M.

Do your own nails. And if you like the look of a French manicure, practice on yourself using one of those French manicure kits.

Salon nails	$20–$30
Home job	free

Advise your maids to do all of the above for themselves as well. They'll save money, and you won't wind up with any beauty nightmares walking down the aisle ahead of you.

As cost-effective as these tips are, you may still find it worth the expense to go for the royal treatment at your beauty salon. In fact, many brides and their bridal parties say the morning spent at the salon enjoying the full bridal package did much to ease their nerves and make them feel more beautiful than if they had done the jobs themselves. They wouldn't trade the experience. Of course there's nothing wrong with that. Your salon may offer you their wedding morning package at a price that's right for you.

You can enjoy the salon treatment for less than the bridal package deal, though. Do you all need facials? It may not be a good idea to have one right before the wedding, in case of irritation. Do you all need pedicures? Massages? Color analysis? Espresso and continental breakfast? Make a deal with the salon owner instead for you to get a group rate for hair stylings and—if you choose—manicures. The package deal you work out for yourself will undoubtedly be much less expensive. One bride negotiated her bridal beauty package down fifty dollars. You could do the same.

An added note: Prepare an emergency kit with clear nail polish, a small sewing kit, aspirin, a nail file, club soda, extra lipstick and face powder, and even a stapler for last-minute mishaps and touch-ups. Have your mother keep it in the car or take it with her to the reception.

41

Gifts for Others

It's always a thoughtful gesture to thank your parents and bridal party for their help with gifts you've chosen just for them. You'll want to get them special gifts that they'll keep forever as a sentimental reminder of your wedding, but since you'll be buying gifts for several people, you'll also want to look for economical choices.

Don't buy the fancy thank-you gifts sold in bridal salons and bridal catalogs. By now you know you can do much better than that.

Look for sales in your local stores, in newspaper and magazine advertisements, even in regular gift catalogs. Try these:

The Body Shop	800-541-2535
CrabTree & Evelyn	800-CRABTREE
Good Catalog Co.	800-225-3870
Hammacher Schlemmer	800-283-9400
Kitchen & Home	800-414-5544
Personal Creations	800-326-6626
Red Rose Collection	800-374-5505
Seasons	800-776-9677
Service Merchandise	800-251-1212
Wireless	800-669-9999

Buy many of the same items (such as frames or gold pens) and negotiate a discount for the group purchase.

Consider gift certificates for makeovers, golf games, lingerie, CDs, even home repair and babysitting services. These, of course, will not be kept forever, but they'll certainly be appreciated as thoughtful gifts. Plus they can be found at low-prices—some for *no* prices.

Several inexpensive gift ideas:

For the Women

sachets	frames	lockets
jewelry	photo albums	clocks

For the Men

wallets	key chains	scarves
gold pen sets	photo albums	clocks

For the Children

jewelry for the ceremony   stuffed animals and toys

Speaking of gifts, do you have insurance for your wedding gifts? The expense is worth it.

Arrange for someone, perhaps your parents, to take your wedding gifts to your home or to theirs after the reception for safekeeping while you're away. This is one of the best forms of insurance known. Never leave your house empty *and* full of new and valuable merchandise.

Have baskets filled with midnight munchies delivered to their hotel rooms after the reception. You can make all the cookies, brownies, and candies yourself and just have a friend make the delivery after you've left for your honeymoon. More rowdy bridal parties who are planning to continue the celebration long into the night will appreciate your sending over several bottles of champagne . . . or the leftovers from the reception!

Not to be dismissed is the handwritten thank-you note. A personal letter is always treasured and is priceless.

42

The Bachelorette Party

Make this celebration an informal affair. You can all go out to a local tavern or restaurant and share the bill. Your bridesmaids may even pick up the tab for you if they choose.

Hold the party at home or at a bridesmaid's house as an economical move.

For a night on the town, provide the responsible services of a designated driver. Instead of the costly limousine, have a nondrinker volunteer for the job. Or you could go by the current trend and just not drink that night.

Another alternative for an even better time: Make it a coed party. Combine the bachelor party with the bachelorette party, and all of you can go out dancing. Besides, no one's left to wonder what the other is up to.

Or don't have a bachelorette party at all. Your shower or the rehearsal dinner may take its place as just a fun night out with your family and friends. Besides, you may want to get some rest before your big day, and you may not want the groom tired, hung over, or stranded far away by devious groomsmen on the morning of the wedding.

43

The Wedding Day
Bridal Brunch

Don't have it catered. While it's good to have some light food available so you and your bridal party and family can get something in your stomachs, there's no need to call in the catering trucks with the big silver trays of quiche and finger sandwiches. Either buy a bag of frozen bagels or a few boxes of rolls and add the fixin's, or plan to cook up some quick light food. No one's going to want to eat very much that morning anyway.

Send some food over to where the groom and his men are getting ready for the ceremony. They have to eat, too. Your brother, the usher, can take some with him when he goes over.

Author's Note

❧

Of course, there are many more ways to save money on your wedding than the ideas mentioned here. You may have near you a fabulous source of materials or flowers, and you may live in a region that offers more moderate prices for wedding services than those of other areas. Yet, although this book cannot give you dates and addresses of the best buys near you, it has taught you to spend your money with quality in mind. It has taught you to protect your investments and to keep organized.

You've become a smarter wedding shopper, and I don't

you'll save plenty of money on your pre-wedding
edding, reception, and honeymoon. All without the
savings showing.

Best of luck on your wedding and in your new life together!

🌿

Index